W9-BOB-802

Waking Up in Winter

Also by Cheryl Richardson

You Can Create an Exceptional Life

The Art of Extreme Self-Care

The Unmistakable Touch of Grace

Stand Up for Your Life

Life Makeovers

Take Time for Your Life

Waking Up in Winter

In Search of What Really
Matters at Midlife

Cheryl Richardson

HarperOne
An Imprint of HarperCollinsPublishers

WAKING UP IN WINTER. Copyright © 2017 by Cheryl Richardson. All rights
reserved. Printed in the United States of America. No part of this book
may be used or reproduced in any manner whatsoever without written
permission except in the case of brief quotations embodied in critical articles
and reviews. For information, address HarperCollins Publishers, 195
Broadway, New York, NY 10007.

HarperCollins books may be purchased for educational, business, or
sales promotional use. For information, please email the Special Markets
Department at SPsales@harpercollins.com.

First HarperOne hardcover published in 2017

FIRST EDITION

Designed by SBI Book Arts, Ltd.

Library of Congress Cataloging-in-Publication Data has been applied for.

ISBN 978−0−06−268166−9

17 18 19 20 21   LSC   10 9 8 7 6 5 4 3 2

For my father,
John Richardson

Contents

Introduction

In September of 2013 I was having dinner with my husband, Michael, and our good friends Bob and Melissa, when Bob happened to mention my next book. "How's the writing going?" he asked, as we enjoyed a predinner drink. "Making much progress?" With a weak smile and a wave of my hand, I attempted to change the subject.

After publishing my sixth self-help book, *You Can Create an Exceptional Life,* with Louise Hay, grande dame of the mind-body-spirit field, I'd spent the better part of the last two years working on my next one, but after pushing through more than a hundred pages, I'd stopped. My heart wasn't in it. Writing was beginning to feel more like homework than creative expression, and I knew I owed my readers and myself more than that. My gut told me to wait, so I'd put the writing on hold. Instead, I turned my attention to the body of work I'd created thus far.

For years I'd maintained a private practice as a professional coach, helping people to improve the quality of their lives. In writing my first two books, *Take Time for Your Life* and *Life Makeovers*, I set out to capture the process I used to help clients deal with the practical, day-to-day issues that kept them stuck in a state of overwhelm and hopelessness. I knew the first thing people needed was to get a handle on the external areas of life that dominated their time and attention. Three years later, after leading a yearlong series for *The Oprah Winfrey Show* and seeing the obstacles that confronted people when they faced change, I wrote my next book, *Stand Up for Your Life*. This time I invited readers to turn their attention inward to develop the qualities of character that would transform fear and self-doubt into personal power. With *The Unmistakable Touch of Grace*, I went beyond the physical and emotional aspects of life and focused on the soul. In this book, I invited readers to cultivate a relationship with the sacred dimension of life by developing spiritual skills like balancing silence with activity and the ability to surrender in the face of fear or confusion in order to gain access to wisdom and insight.

Reviewing what I'd written helped me to understand my ambivalence about starting a new book. Truth be told, I not only felt like I'd said all I needed to say about how to create a meaningful, fulfilling life, but I also lacked the motivation to write another self-help book. I wasn't interested in adding to the avalanche of advice that was filling my inbox and news feed nearly every day. Something had shifted in me, and I felt like an established author with a loyal following who wrote a popular blog but had nothing more to say in a book.

Or so it seemed.

Back at dinner my friend Bob pressed on. "Come on, kiddo! When are we going get something to read?"

I took a deep breath, ready to launch into a litany of excuses, when my husband said something interesting: "You know, one thing you've always found time to do is write in your journal. Why don't you publish that? You love May Sarton, and maybe it's your turn to spill the beans about the intimate life of a creative woman, but this time in the twenty-first century."

May Sarton became an important influence for me after I read her book *Journal of a Solitude*. First published in 1973, it gave the reader access to the private diary of a creative woman who expressed herself through poetry, fiction, and nonfiction. I'd stumbled upon her journal a decade later at a small town fair as I sifted through used books piled high on tables. By age twelve I'd become a voracious reader and a devoted journal keeper, and the prospect of exploring another writer's life was irresistible.

From the very first page of *Journal of a Solitude*, I felt a kindred connection with Sarton. A keen observer of life, she wrote passionately and artistically about the world around her. Morning dew blanketing the grass in her backyard, a vase full of daffodils bathed in sunlight on her desk, or a glistening tomato freshly picked from the garden—these ordinary snapshots of life took on new meaning under her poetic scrutiny. In addition to capturing the beauty of her surroundings, Sarton was also fiercely honest about her inner world. Throughout the journal she confessed her irritation at the demands of managing a busy household, her sadness at not being properly recognized for her work, and her frustration at navigating the tricky business of being a private woman with a public life. Sarton went on to write a series of journals, and when I finished one I turned eagerly to the next.

Michael was right. During my struggles to craft a new book, I never stopped keeping a journal. Since childhood I've been hungry to understand myself and the world around me, and writing has been my vehicle for that exploration. Writing comforts me. It connects my head and my heart, allowing me access to hidden feelings and new perspectives. I write to make sense of the inner chaos I experience at times and to make the unconscious conscious. By processing my daily life on the page, I open myself up to insights that heal and support my growth. Keeping a journal also helps me to stay tethered to my inner life, especially when my outer life feels hectic or overwhelming.

Now, staring at my husband across the dinner table, I was surprised by the sudden rush of excitement that filled my body. Could this be the next evolution of my work—giving readers an inside look at how I actually *live* a life dedicated to growth and healing? Might this format be a welcomed change? In my weekly blog, I'd made the shift from offering how-to advice to sharing personal stories about the ways in which I was doing my best to live a more authentic life, and readers had responded favorably. I did it because I wanted people to know they weren't alone, and that in spite of my having become a recognized authority in the self-help world, the truth was I struggled, too.

Within moments of considering the idea, however, my enthusiasm gave way to doubt. Who would want to read about my daily life? What could I possibly teach readers in a journal? And even if I could pull it off, did I really want to make myself so vulnerable? What if my most intimate thoughts were met by criticism or ridicule? Or, nearly as bad, what if the book was ignored?

I spent a few days mulling over the idea, and as I did, my doubts gradually receded. Publishing a journal would give me a chance to teach by example. It would allow me to show readers how to learn from life, how to use day-to-day experiences as a catalyst for growth and empowerment. And it would also give me a chance to share the tools, support, and resources I use myself.

So it was that I decided to follow May Sarton's lead. Inspired in a way I hadn't been in a long time, I went to work, and my renewed appetite for writing told me I was on the right track.

That's how this book was born.

One of the great advantages of keeping a journal is that it provides a way to reflect on our lives. After doing this for more than forty years, I'm still surprised by how a messy, nonlinear process can provide such clarity and perspective. While at the time I had no idea where this particular journal would lead, it's clear to me now that these pages tell the story of what happened when I made the decision to move on from writing self-help, and in doing so discovered that there was something much bigger going on. A new awareness of my mortality had set in, and it caused me to begin reevaluating everything—my work, my marriage, my friendships, and my priorities—in that light. Years of success left me feeling grateful and blessed, but as I entered my fifties, I started to feel something else: anxious and unsettled. Was I really happy? Did I still feel stimulated and satisfied with my work? Now that the finish line of life was creeping closer, was I really living or just going through the motions?

This is the existential world I entered as I began this journal in the middle of a busy speaking schedule. While my aim was to chronicle my experiences in present time, I've chosen to include some background information now and then to provide helpful context. This book is an honest account of what happened when I started listening to my life.

At some point, we're all invited to take the hero's journey—to leave familiar territory, face our demons, travel through the darkness, and find our way to a better life, one more aligned with who we've become. I invite you to take this journey with me. Whether you're questioning your own mortality, dealing with a life crisis, hungry to feel more alive, or just plain tired of going through the motions because you know, deep in your heart, you're meant for something more, it's my hope that the challenges, lessons, and desires I explore here will strike a resonant chord within you. While the hero's journey is a solitary adventure, it's comforting to know we're not alone.

So, with a nod of gratitude to my muse, May Sarton, I set this journal in motion with the same words she used to start her own some four decades ago . . .

Begin here.

Waking Up
in Winter

September 30th

I woke this morning to a cool breeze drifting through the bedroom window. *It's starting,* I thought. *Winter will be here before you know it.* Seems like only yesterday I was mixing compost and soil in pots on the deck, poring over flowers at the local greenhouse, and balancing on the ladder in the basement to turn the water back on for the outdoor faucet. Life hurtles by, days turning into weeks turning into months, and now the seasons I love most—the blossoming of spring, lazy summer days, and the fiery beauty of autumn—are coming to an end. Looking out the window at my withering garden, I long for time to slow down, but I know better. It's not about time; it's about me. I need to plant my feet in the present moment. Time rushes by when I'm not where I am.

Fortunately, I took a vacation this summer and reveled in the spaciousness and freedom of a clear calendar. As the days passed, I started keeping a list of what made me happy so I'd remember when life got busy again:

Lying in bed listening to birdsong

Cooking a new, healthy recipe

Slipping into a cozy bed warmed by a heating pad

Watching Poupon wrestle with catnip

Long walks with Michael, lost in conversation

Waking up at sunrise

Getting a foot massage

Leisurely shopping for clothes

Creating new music playlists

Sitting on the deck watching hummingbirds dance in the air

These are the little things I dream about doing during long car rides to the airport, or when staring out the window of an airplane, traveling to yet another city to speak. I'm growing tired of hearing myself say I'm looking forward to (fill in the blank), followed by a bittersweet sadness rising in my chest. I need to stop looking ahead and start asking: What am I doing *now* that keeps me looking forward to something else? And why am I doing it?

I'm preoccupied with how I spend my time these days, and I can trace the source of this feeling to my fiftieth birthday nearly four years ago. That morning I went downstairs, got on the treadmill, and began to watch a movie on TV. At the first commercial break, I realized I had no idea what the story was about as the significance of this birthday hit me full on. Fifty years old. Midlife. More years behind me than lay ahead. I'd heard all the clichés before, but they always applied to someone else—parents, aunts and uncles, older friends.

Now they belonged to me.

Rather than avoid the subject of dying, I made a decision to dive into it. I shut the TV off and started thinking: *What will life be like when I'm in my eighties or nineties, if I live that long? Will I enjoy good health or spend my days slumped over in a nursing-home chair? Who will handle my things when I die—my journals and the cards and letters I've stashed away in the old cedar trunk in the garage? Will I outlive Michael, my family members, and my friends? How old will I be when I finally leave the planet?*

I thought about what I'd regret not having done before I died, and a few answers immediately sprang to mind:

Live peacefully in my body

Make beauty and nature more of a priority in my everyday life

Be less defended and more open to others

Let go of my self-consciousness and be bolder with my choices

These regrets may not be typical bucket-list items, but they reflect what's always been deeply important to me: the inner adventure. I'm passionate about self-development and challenging myself to grow as a person, seeking out experiences that contribute to the evolution of my soul. Before I pushed the reality of mortality back into the shadowy corners of my consciousness, I had to admit that frightening as it was to think about my expiration date, it was strangely comforting as well. Death isn't wishy-washy. It doesn't fool around. When I'm done, I'm done (with this life, anyway), so I'd better make damn sure I'm doing what I really want to do right now.

October 1st

It's a cool morning, and the sun is making a feeble attempt to penetrate the clouds. As I'm sitting on the deck writing, I notice a crooked black V taking shape in the distant sky. A flock of geese is on the wing, and soon they'll be heading south. Another sign that winter is drawing near. Time off this summer has deepened my love affair with the outdoors, and I'll miss lying in the backyard watching red-tailed hawks gliding in the wind or staring at woodchucks as they gobble up the clover in our lawn outside the living-room window.

Today I have time. Space. Freedom to meander, to think, to be. After breakfast, I slipped out the front door to trim the rose bushes that line the shrubs by the driveway. Gardening settles me. My mind quiets as I steady myself in the here and now. No worries about going somewhere or getting things done. Just present-moment magic. I love pruning flowers, encouraging and supporting their growth, contributing to the beauty that surrounds our home.

Once I tidied up the roses, I moved to the backyard to prune the tall butterfly bushes that host lemon-yellow swallowtails and my precious monarchs. Countless drooping brown blossoms needed my attention. Not yet ready to level the bush in preparation for winter, I pruned only the dead flowers and left its sturdy limbs intact. I'll do the end-of-season trimming another day.

Gardening, like life, requires courage. We must be brave enough to cut back the old and sit with bare branches, awaiting new growth. And we must trust that it will come.

October 2nd

Tomorrow Michael and I leave for two weeks of travel overseas. As much as I look forward to teaching, seeing old friends, and feasting on the beauty of European architecture, I'm back to dealing with packing, long security lines, and waiting, waiting, waiting. On the one hand, I feel fortunate to teach what I love, to travel to beautiful places, and to know that my words have impact and meaning for many. Most people yearn for this sense of purpose in their own lives, and I'm grateful to have found it in mine. But my gratitude is tempered by the physical and emotional exhaustion I feel as a result of living this way. There's a subtle rumbling below the surface of my life, tremors that signal the need for change. Lately, when teaching, I find myself repeating something Thomas (my first coach) told me during one of our early sessions: "Life gives you messages," he warned, "and if you don't get the message, you'll get a lesson. If you don't learn the lesson, you're sure to get a problem, and if you don't handle the problem, you'll get a full-blown crisis."

The anxiety that starts brewing a week before my next trip, the irritation I feel when lugging the faded blue suitcase out of the closet, or the slight pulling away from Michael in an effort to temper my sadness, are all messages. And I need to pay attention.

Fortunately, on this trip I won't have to contend with missing Michael. He'll be by my side most of the time, and having him with me will keep me centered and happy. He's reasonable and calm, and he knows how to make me laugh when I need it most.

Okay, time to stop writing and start packing.

October 4th

I've arrived in London to begin my speaking tour, and it feels good to be unpacked and settled in our hotel room. I'm looking forward to seeing friends, visiting gardens, and people watching, in spite of having a crazy schedule while here. In the next ten days, I'm set to give talks in several cities, including Hamburg, Salzburg, and London, and I hope the travel angels stay close. Michael is snoring softly in the next room, and for once the familiar sound makes me smile. I've missed having him with me on the road.

The rooms in this hotel are small but cozy, and I woke this morning inspired to create a little nest for myself so I could write. I have a cup of hot tea with honey on the coffee table next to me, and I've positioned the love seat to face the largest of the hotel windows, which provides a panoramic view of the neighborhood. The late-season flowers spilling over their window boxes, weathered brick chimneys, and even the grinning stone gargoyles are perfect company.

I'm relieved to be back in the flow of writing again. This intimacy of journal keeping gives me energy, and I find myself excited to put pen to paper. If my sweet friend Debbie Ford were here, she'd congratulate me for taking a creative risk and following my heart. As I write, I can sense her staunch support from the other side. It has been eight months since she passed, and rarely a day goes by when I don't feel the blunt ache of loss deep in my chest. It still catches me by surprise when I reach for the phone to call her, or look forward to the next time we'll laugh together like schoolgirls in a hotel where we're both scheduled to speak.

Grief is like the ocean with its never-ending waves. Since Debbie's death I've been swimming in the pain of this loss, feeling steady one minute and unstable the next. As I've surrendered to the heartache, though, and allowed the sadness to flow through me, I've noticed that with each wave, a piece of sorrow gets washed away, leaving behind precious memories of our time together. These days I'm focusing less on the pain and more on the profound influence this woman had on my life.

Debbie was an extraordinary soul. We met fifteen years ago at the Boston Park Plaza hotel. I was sitting at a round table having breakfast with a group of fellow authors, when the event director brought Debbie over and introduced us. I'd heard of Debbie's shadow work based on Jungian psychology, and, curious to learn more, I decided to attend her talk. On the morning of Debbie's workshop, I slipped into the back of the room and was instantly captivated. Slim, graceful, and completely at ease onstage, Debbie sauntered back and forth, her dark eyes sparkling, her presence filling the room with an electric energy. She spoke openly and with great compassion about subjects most people shy away from: the pain of childhood trauma and abuse; feelings of envy and jealousy; our human tendency to judge people harshly, especially ourselves; and the corrosive shame that limits our ability to fully express our deepest desires.

As I watched, Debbie skillfully challenged the audience to own both the good and the bad within themselves, the saint and the sinner, in order to realize their full potential. Embracing the light *and* the dark is the key to living a rich life, she promised. And when she finished her introductory comments, she asked us to sit back, close our eyes, and prepare to discover a priceless gift.

I thought about sneaking out of the room, something I'd typically do for fear of being vulnerable in public, especially given that I'd be speaking at this conference later in the day myself. But something told me to stay. As I sat quietly in the back of the hall, I closed my eyes and let myself be guided by Debbie's soothing voice. I felt like she was speaking directly to me. She asked me to breathe slowly into my heart for several minutes before inviting me to think about someone from my past whose behavior I found hurtful or upsetting. Immediately a business associate I'd been involved with a few years earlier came to mind, someone I came to dislike for being greedy.

Next, Debbie asked us to explore our experience of this person in detail. How did he or she behave? What exactly did he or she say? What did this person do that made him or her so unlikable? I didn't need to look far for the answer: this man had taken up too much space in our conversations; he'd made *his* needs a priority in every meeting, and he'd expected people around him to meet those needs without resistance.

Debbie then invited me to find this person inside myself. I flashed back to a little girl grabbing an extra dinner roll from the dining room table and hiding it under her napkin. A wave of shame washed over me, and this memory led to another: I'd taken a blouse from my mother's closet and hidden it in my bedroom. Just touching the blouse made me feel special, like a grown-up, and I wanted more of that feeling.

Lastly, Debbie encouraged us to consider how this seemingly unforgivable part of ourselves might actually be a gift in disguise—a quality that, when embraced, might serve us somehow in the present. That's when the force of her work hit me, and I started to cry.

Until that point, my professional career had been centered on self-care strategies—the art of making one's needs and desires a top priority. My books and workshops were based on these topics, and I was starting to feel like a hypocrite. A busy travel schedule and regular appearances on television were pushing the limits of my own ability to set boundaries, and I was feeling chronically exhausted and overwhelmed.

As I explored my emotional reaction to my greedy colleague, I suddenly understood—in a way that transcends knowing—that he did, in fact, have something profound to teach me. I needed to embrace my own greediness if I wanted to regain some balance and peace in my life. I had to stop denying the existence of that greedy girl and welcome her instead. I needed her to step in and teach my adult woman a thing or two about speaking up, asking for what she wanted, and getting her needs met.

Those twenty minutes changed my life. Not only did I walk out of the room with the courage and confidence to set limits on my time and energy, I left knowing that I'd found a soul sister. Debbie and I shared lunch that afternoon, and sure enough, it launched a friendship that flourished over the next decade and a half.

No wonder Debbie has been on my mind. I'm doing it to myself again. I've been traveling nonstop, running my business from the road while trying to write, and I'm worn out. I thought I had this self-care thing figured out, but now I'm not so sure. It's an ongoing process, this personal growth, and it's never straightforward or linear. We spiral in and out of the shadowy places, doing our best to move toward the light, only to find ourselves back where we started. I need to reengage that greedy little girl again and let her help me create more balance in my life. I need more time with Michael, I need rest, and I need the comfort and care of my domestic daily routine. I want to feel alive instead of frustrated and exhausted most of the time. Otherwise what's the point?

Which brings me back to my little nest here in London and the birth of this journal. I look forward to being home for a while once my end-of-year trips are over so I can embark on a new kind of journey. Autumn will soon give way to winter, the perfect time to hole up and explore the inner world. I need to take stock, to heed the messages that have been calling out for my attention, to get off this spinning wheel and reevaluate my life. I'm curious to discover what dwells deep down in the murky realms of myself. Perhaps once the sediment churned up by my busy life has settled I'll see it more clearly.

For now, however, we're off to Germany.

October 5th

I'm in Hamburg to speak at a conference. I came into the hotel restaurant this morning hoping to find some breakfast, but the staff was already taking away the buffet. In need of sustenance for the busy day ahead, I pleaded for protein, and a sympathetic hostess went to the kitchen and returned with a bowl of hard-boiled eggs. They'll do nicely.

She also brought a treat. When delivering my tea, she included three little pots of honey, each a different flavor: wildflower, lavender, and heather. It's things like this—simple, delightful pleasures—that interrupt an old pattern of mine, where I look for what's wrong when I'm traveling, instead of what's right. The unexpected kindness of a stranger in a foreign land feels especially comforting and sweet.

I'm scheduled to give two magazine interviews and record a video in advance of a workshop I'll be teaching here next year. I've given so many media interviews that talking about myself bores me, but I'll do my best to mix things up and make them fun.

Later

One interview down. A young woman who looked to be in her late twenties gazed at me hopefully, her face searching mine for answers. "Is it really okay to make caring for ourselves a priority?" she asked. "Won't some people be offended by that behavior?"

It turns out that the term *self-care* is difficult to translate to German. It sounds selfish to the native ear, she tells me, and she's afraid that people will think I'm suggesting they behave in ways that might appear self-absorbed or arrogant. God knows I've heard this before. We might be in Germany, but her fear is universal. Men, women, young, old, no matter where I travel I'm confronted with the same question: *"Isn't teaching people to practice better self-care teaching them to be selfish?"*

Yes it is, I usually agree, and that's a good thing.

Most of the people who read my books, attend my talks, or follow me on social media admit that they've spent a ridiculous amount of time trying to manage the perceptions of others by being nice. They say yes when a quiet voice inside whispers, *No, no, no.* They attempt to defend the boundaries they set, and in doing so open doors that invite arguments and eventual backtracking. When they start to make their own needs a priority, it often rocks the boat they've been delicately balancing for years. As a result, the people around them get upset and start questioning the new behavior because change feels scary and unsettling to the safe and familiar tribe.

When I give people the tools they need to take better care of themselves—the language to say no, permission to gracefully disappoint others, strategies for setting firm boundaries that honor one's time and energy, for instance—it *can* appear selfish at first. But here's the thing: I'm encouraging people to honor the soul, not the ego. In reality, good soul-care fosters integrity. It means telling the truth and making choices from love rather than guilt or obligation, thereby strengthening relationships all around.

Of course, there's a deeper cultural dynamic at work here, one that has been set in place for centuries. We cannot be controlled if we develop a mind of our own, a desire for freedom, and health, and personal power. It *is* empowering to practice good self-care, and the tribes we belong to may not like it. Those tribes might take the form of our marriage, family, employers, political establishments, or religious organizations. Tribes tend to resist change, and people who are empowered don't go along to get along.

"No worries," I tell my interviewer, as we continue our discussion. At first glance self-care may appear to be selfish, but without caring for our own needs we're incapable of experiencing true, authentic connections with ourselves and others. And ultimately that's what we all long for. We just go about it in the wrong way, by people-pleasing and stifling our own desires.

When we finish the interview, I walk away thinking about my own self-care. I began my career by teaching what I needed to learn, and now that I've learned it, I need to remember it. Selfish is good. Paying attention to what my soul needs and doing something about it is the key to getting back on track. And I need to get back on track. I'm growing weary of the road, of my life, really, and I feel like I'm losing a vital connection to myself. There are signs of system overload, the beginning of a descent.

For years I've told my coaching clients that all positive change begins with telling the truth. "Don't worry about what you'll do with the truth," I'd explain, "just start naming it." And sure enough, once they'd talk about what wasn't working in their lives, I'd watch the Universe line up doorways that opened at the most opportune times, making it easier to take the actions that would honor their real needs and desires. They just had to align their energy with truth.

So what's my truth? What isn't working anymore? Where might I need an open door?

I don't feel good in my body. Although I've started walking and have lost some weight, traveling makes it difficult to stay on track. I don't sleep well in hotels, and I end up feeling exhausted more often than not. Eating is a challenge, too. I find myself using sweets for comfort while on the road and it not only leaves me feeling moody and physically sluggish, but I'm also tortured by the way I beat myself up for not being more disciplined and committed to my health. It's a constant reminder of what I said I'd regret most when I considered my own death.

I miss the kind of connection Michael and I shared before life got so crazy. We loved being together, taking road trips, going to movies, or lying in bed talking and laughing late into the night. Now I'm constantly bracing myself against leaving and it's created too much emotional distance between us. I also miss the comfort of cuddling with our little guy, Poupon, waking up in my own bed, and being present for the changing beauty of the land where we live.

I long for the days when I had the space in my schedule to enjoy leisurely time alone or to visit with good friends. Instead, as soon as I'm home, I'm psychologically preparing myself for the next trip and playing catch-up with the work that's piled up in my office. And then there's my work. As much as I hate to admit it, I also feel bored with some of what I do now. I crave new creative outlets, deeper conversations with students, and the chance to teach from home without losing the intimate face-to-face connection that traveling affords me. These days I wake under a cloud of sadness that follows me throughout the day, and it casts a dreary shadow on everything I do.

Now there's a truth that's hard to admit.

As I read over the last few paragraphs, I think about all the women I've listened to over the years who are quick to dismiss their frustration at being so busy and overwhelmed because they compare themselves to those who are less fortunate. I, too, fear I might sound like a whining ingrate. Shouldn't I feel blessed to live the kind of life most people dream of? Who am I to complain when I'm fortunate enough to have people read my books or pay good money to hear me speak? Isn't this the life I said I wanted, the one I've worked so hard to create?

26

Like it or not, something has to give. Sustaining the status quo is weakening my emotional immune system, and my confidence and trust in myself is getting depleted. And without this inner strength, it's too easy to keep giving in to what's safe and familiar rather than make the changes I know I need to make. And then there's the little problem of not knowing what to do. So I keep traveling and teaching in spite of the cost.

I'm a coach, for crying out loud, and I help people make positive changes in their lives all the time. I don't know why I feel so stuck. This feels different. Bigger. More about determining the direction of my life than shuffling a few priorities. How do I get myself out from under the success I've spent the last twenty-five years building without losing what I've created? And where do I go from here?

At this point, what I do know is that in order to rebuild my emotional and physical immune system, I need rest, space, silence, and, I suspect, to sit with not knowing for a while. When and how to make this happen is the question.

October 7th

We returned to London from Germany last night and went right to bed. I've stayed at this boutique hotel before, so it feels homey and familiar. There's a hair salon across the street, a

Starbucks on the corner (seems they're everywhere!), and a grocery store within walking distance—the conveniences of home.

Michael and I are having a good time. Our togetherness on this trip is making me painfully aware of how adept I've become at tolerating our separation. For years I've put responsibility ahead of desire, and it's left me with well-developed suck-it-up muscles. These muscles have allowed me to let my anxiety about leaving Poupon with others get the best of me rather than press to make suitable arrangements for Michael and me to be together. Normally I feel less anxious when I'm away knowing that Michael is keeping the home fires burning and taking care of Poupon, but this time our dear friends Robin and Larry have offered to house-sit. Fortunately, they know Poupon (and the house), and will no doubt take good care of both. They've also offered to make themselves available for future trips, and I want to make more use of their kindness. I never really allow myself to fully experience the pleasures of a new place because it doesn't feel right without Michael. So today I'm choosing to visit all my favorite places with him by my side.

We sleep late, and when we finally get dressed we decide to go for an afternoon walk before heading out to dinner with our friends Robert and Hollie, who live in the Chiswick district of London. In search of flowers to bring with us, we wind up in Covent Garden, one of my favorite places because it reminds me of the old Faneuil Hall in Boston. The space is full of light and life, with tall glass ceilings that open to the sky and crowds of shoppers weaving in and out of tables filled with antique jewelry, handmade pocketbooks, and festive hats. At the end of this cavernous space, patrons spill out into courtyards that host performance artists making magic, and little kids smile.

As we stroll past tables, combing them for treasures, I'm delighted to rediscover the little statues I purchased for friends a few years back, small figurines of kings and queens, animals and birds made with such convincing detail that I half expected them to step forward and introduce themselves. I haven't seen them on recent visits, and I'm eager to grab some for gifts.

The two women behind the counter are just closing up when we arrive, but their round faces beam a welcome in unison, like sunflowers opening to the light. In no time we pick out a handful of riches—a blue whale with a shy smile, a proud turkey with feathers in full bloom, a knight in gleaming armor, and a goofy, saucer-eyed cat. When several other last-minute customers show up we offer to wrap our own purchases, and you would think we'd offered to pay double. "You've turned a bad day around with your kindness!" one of the women exclaims. "We've had a valuable item stolen today, and we've been terribly upset."

It's funny how little things can inspire such gratitude. For me, it's flavored honey; for this kind woman behind the counter, it's bubble-wrapping customers. Michael responds with characteristic grace. "Well, that makes us even happier to be able to make these purchases," he tells the woman. I love his good heart (I wrote "god heart" at first, and the misspelling seems apropos).

Later

Dinner with Robert and Hollie tonight was so much fun. I love Robert and think of him as a soul brother. During our meal, I told the story of how our connection was forged last August. When I'm traveling, I've learned to connect with people who share my desire for deeper, more soulful conversations and experiences to make being away from home a bit easier. Robert, a fellow author and traveler, is one of those friends. Our relationship grew when he turned out to be presenting at the same two conferences in Australia that I was last year. By the time we got to Sydney, we were both so homesick that we slipped away from the downtown hotel for a stroll through the Royal Botanic Garden to talk about our loved ones.

As we passed a small bamboo forest, Robert's cell phone rang. It was his two-year-old son, Christopher, calling to hear his father's voice. Robert was doing his best to help Christopher understand the concept of travel, which was sweet until I heard him say, "No, Christopher, Daddy's not in the next room." I walked away to hide the tears that sprang to my eyes when I saw the pained look on Robert's face. I knew that feeling. The two weeks that loomed before I could see Michael again felt like an eternity.

I can see now that my emotional reaction to Robert's conversation with his son was another message, my soul's way of trying to get my attention. If tears could talk, they would have told me, *You miss Michael more than you realize and you need to be home. All this traveling is too much, and it's time to cut back.* I didn't get the message then, because I wasn't ready to listen. Instead, I did my best to suck it up by staying busy. Denial by distraction.

During that trip, Robert and I got together from time to time in mutual support. We enjoyed foot-reflexology treatments, drank green juice, and consumed doses of local beauty whenever possible. Good self-care on the road. One night on our way back from dinner, we walked past Sydney's St. Mary's Cathedral, a gorgeous Gothic structure that evoked my early Catholic-school days when I was required to attend Mass every day. A ten-year-old angel in training, I'd sit upright in the pew, black patent leather shoes positioned properly on the kneeler, prayerful hands folded in my lap. My eyes were always pinned to the stained-glass windows, towering kaleidoscopes that pulled me into their mysterious, spiritual world. The beauty I devoured in church ignited a love affair with sacred space that made a visit to the cathedral, decades later, impossible to resist.

But there was more. As we reminisced about the story over dinner tonight, I was reminded of something Marion Woodman, the Jungian analyst, told me long ago: "Pay attention to the images that show up in your dreams, or the ones from everyday life that stay with you. These images often hold clues to unconscious material that's attempting to rise to the surface." The towering cathedral in Sydney is one of those images, and I made a mental note to find a picture of it so I can keep it in view. I suspect it represents something important that's related to this time in my life.

Being with Robert and Hollie was all the richer for our shared love of the Enneagram, a common language that brings our conversations to a deep, nourishing level very quickly. I'd been introduced to the Enneagram more than twenty years earlier when a friend referred me to Helen Palmer's work. A prominent teacher in the field, Palmer described the Enneagram as a human-development system consisting of nine personality types, each with its own "distinct, well-developed coping strategy for relating to self, others, and the environment. In addition, each of the nine types has its own precise path to psychological and spiritual freedom." Back then I was drawn to her work but had other more pressing interests, so I merely touched the surface.

Years later, Robert introduced me to it again, this time by inviting me to take a test developed by Don Richard Riso and Russ Hudson, authors of a book called *The Wisdom of the Enneagram*. After spending nearly an hour online answering multiple questions to determine my type, I discovered I was a 2—the Helper. Once I knew this, I went to the book and fell in love with Riso and Hudson's work.

By the time I'd finished reading about my type, I felt a strange combination of exposed and deeply understood.

The chapter about the Helper told the story of my life. It described my childhood experience, my history of sacrificing my needs in relationships in the hopes of gaining love, my propensity for people-pleasing, and my bullying behavior when I felt unappreciated and resentful. It also captured the essence of what I love doing when I'm in a healthy, balanced state—supporting those in need without an agenda and helping people to realize their full potential. These are the gifts the Helper has to offer, and providing them brings me immense joy and satisfaction.

As I write this, I suddenly understand what the image of St. Mary's Cathedral represents. Seeing myself through the lens of the Helper was a pivotal experience that forced me to question deeply held beliefs about my reason for being on the planet, many of which were rooted in my early Catholic-school training. While I've taken on the challenge of over-giving in my own life and built a career out of teaching self-care, there's still a young girl inside me who believes that her life should be devoted to others. She learned early on that selfless service is the way to live a righteous, spiritual life; that it's honorable to focus on others at the expense of herself; and that a ticket to heaven is only offered to charitable souls who dedicate their lives to those in need. She's superstitious, anxious about getting her own needs met, and feels unworthy of love without giving something in return.

As I rethink my life, I need to pay attention to her. While my understanding of the Enneagram has given me permission to make the evolution of my own soul a top priority, she may have another agenda that could derail my efforts.

In addition to helping me understand myself better, the Enneagram also changed my relationship with Michael. After taking the test himself, he discovered he was a type 5, the Investigator, and when we put our profiles together, it gave us an instant appreciation for the friction points and gifts in our relationship. Things that often bothered me—Michael's habit of always presenting both sides of an issue, his tendency to overthink things, and his need for privacy and time alone—suddenly took on new meaning and context. I could begin to see how those qualities supported the development of what I love most about him—his compassionate heart, his visionary thinking, and his ability to focus on and stick with a project for long stretches at a time.

Dinner had hardly begun at Robert and Hollie's when the four of us launched into a discussion about the Enneagram and how it had impacted our lives, our work, and our relationships. This was my first chance to spend real time with Hollie, and I'm so glad I did. She's deep and wise, and her thoughtful words are infused with truth and beauty. She's the kind of person I want to slip into my back pocket and take with me on my travels so we can enjoy long conversations over tea.

I feel grateful for these friendships—for people who live vertically rather than just skim the surface of life, and who appreciate the give-and-take of meaningful conversation. This evening made me realize how much I value true peers—friends on the path who are committed to the evo-lution of their own consciousness, and to cultivating soulful connections with others. The Enneagram paved the way for an authentic, down-to-earth experience tonight, and I leave knowing that I want the time and energy to invest in more of these relationships back home. When I have true friends to share my life with (something the Helper values most), I don't need much else to be happy.

October 9th

I'm sitting in the dining room at Claridge's hotel waiting for my friend Ileen to arrive. She uses this hotel for most of her meetings, and I can see why. It's a classic, old-world establish-ment with doormen dressed in top hats and long, cashmere coats; lush bouquets of in-season flowers placed throughout; and a grand, sweeping staircase that begs for photographs and a royal entrance. Such beauty! We're having breakfast together, and I've arrived early to spend a little time writing before she gets here.

Meeting Ileen a few years ago was like being introduced to the Enneagram, another life-changing event for both Michael and me. Friends made the introduction thinking that it would be fruitful for us to talk about movie and TV projects. Ileen and I scheduled a visit in the middle of the summer of 2009, and over the course of several days we spent hours talking about our lives, our work, and our desire to make art that raises consciousness.

Ileen greets life with the wide-eyed enthusiasm of a child visiting Disneyland for the very first time. She has piercing blue eyes, a mane of silver curls, and a booming voice that commands attention. There were so many things I instantly liked—her energy and enthusiasm for life, her sharp mind, the breadth of her experience, and her wicked sense of humor. After spending the evenings with us, Michael felt the same way. "I think she might be soul family," I said to him as we watched Ileen get swallowed up by the airport doors on the night she left. "I think you're right," he agreed, "She feels like the sister I never had."

It's heartening to realize that I can form meaningful friendships later in life, the kind that feel like family. Maturity makes it easy to drop pretense—a benefit of aging. I love meeting someone who's empowered, comfortable in her skin, direct about who she is and what she wants, and willing to share from the heart. Gone are the days of playing games in my relationships, tolerating cocktail-level conversations and people who take and rarely give. I also have no interest in minimizing my power or intellect to prevent someone from feeling threatened or uncomfortable.

Well, I say those days are gone, but not quite. Instead, what I realize as I write is that Ileen has the kind of confidence in herself and clarity about what she wants that I admire, especially during a time when I feel a bit wobbly and unsure of myself. I just need to keep listening to my life. I need to pay attention to what I know to be true and I'll get clear about what I want. Then I have to trust that I can make it happen.

Yesterday Michael and I slept in, and when I woke first, I made myself a cup of tea and settled in to write. I treasure my mornings alone, although it's been a little tricky having them to myself while traveling together in a new time zone. Back home it's quite different. Michael is a night owl, and has been since he was a teenager. He goes to bed around 6 a.m., and wakes up in the afternoon. When he was a kid he managed to get through school with limited sleep and a knack for test taking, and as an adult he found jobs that allowed him to work at night. I, on the other hand, have always been a morning person. I love going to bed around 10 p.m. so I can rise with the sun. Although Michael and I have found a way to make things work, it wasn't easy.

Marriage is the ultimate spiritual school, something I was forewarned of years ago when studying the work of Harville Hendrix, a master at teaching couples and families how to use relationships to promote personal transformation. Harville explained, "Every partnership is a spiritual union that offers us a chance to grow. You can be assured you'll marry the person who will be *incapable* of meeting your most important needs, and that's when the journey begins." I laughed out loud when I heard him say this, but also shuddered inside at the truth of his words. At the time, Michael and I were struggling to make our opposing sleep schedules work.

Sharing daylight hours certainly felt like a "most important need" to me, but Michael didn't seem willing or able to meet it. The conflict was taking a toll on our marriage.

Harville was right. My relationship with Michael has single-handedly been the most potent force for growth in my life thus far. And most growth spurts have been initiated by trouble in paradise. Two years ago the difference in our sleep schedules seemed like an insurmountable obstacle. I wanted Michael to play with on weekends. I resented having to handle the management of the household and our daily lives. I was tired of making excuses for why Michael couldn't be with me during daytime family events. And I was fed up with worrying about what other people were thinking about our unusual setup.

Resentment would build; I'd complain; and Michael would do his best to change his behavior, even seeing a sleep specialist at one point to create some kind of transition plan. But the plan didn't stick. Eventually his body would go right back to its unique circadian rhythm, and we'd start fighting all over again. Every day felt like a battle between what I wanted (Michael and a normal sleep schedule) and reality (I was married to a vampire).

There were some days when I wondered about whether or not we could make our relationship work with such different schedules. Months of pent-up frustration began to take a toll, and the tension of not getting my needs met felt intolerable. Looking back, I can see that allowing myself to even think about a breakup was a way of relieving the pressure I felt because in my mind, the situation was hopeless. So I kept shoving my feelings under the rug in the hopes that things would miraculously work themselves out, and that's when something beautiful happened. An ordinary moment inspired me to stop railing against reality.

One morning on my way to the bathroom, I stopped to watch Michael sleeping. He was lying on his right side, hands together under his head as if in prayer. It was a position I'd seen hundreds of times before, but this time felt different. As I watched his chest slowly rise and fall with each breath, my heart softened. *He's my husband,* I thought to myself. *My best friend. My lover. My playmate.* From our very first date I knew Michael was special, a man whose principles and integrity are reflected in the way he conducts his life. Loving and kind, his sensitivity promotes both an allegiance to beauty and a natural tendency to treat people with respect. These qualities matter deeply to me, not to mention that he makes me laugh, every single day.

To hell with living a conventional life and following society's norms, I decided as I stared at his sweet, resting face. *We'll make our own rules from now on.* And we did. I gave up the fight, Michael breathed a sigh of relief, and we set out to create a new kind of partnership, a union that supports us both creatively and intimately. Michael writes at night. I write in the early morning. We plan date nights *and* days. And so far it's working.

It's strange how one seemingly ordinary moment in time can settle years of arguments and angst. I suspect it's a testament to the power of mature love and a commitment to soul growth. There are some things in life worth surrendering for.

As I sit here writing about this now, I recognize something important. The decision to shape our marriage in our own way was a brave choice that challenged the rules we were raised by, both in our families and in society. We're all deeply influenced in conscious and unconscious ways by the tribes we're born into, and it takes courage and great strength to challenge the norm—to marry outside one's religion or culture, to live in another part of the world, or to choose to make art instead of following a family legacy in a more conventional profession, for instance. Now that Michael and I have tackled such a big challenge and created our own new and improved tribal rules, I wonder what others might need to be rewritten in order to live more authentically. I need to talk with him about this.

October 10th

This morning, after I finished writing and Michael dressed, we went for a stroll on the streets of London. As we stepped out of the hotel, I smiled up at the sun, feeling grateful for the cloudless autumn afternoon. Weaving in and out of the crowds, I grabbed Michael's arm as we headed for Shaftesbury Avenue. I was excited to introduce him to Monmouth Coffee, a ritual for me when I come to London on my own. Monmouth is a tiny shop where you have to suck in your stomach to squeeze by the long line of customers who've already placed their orders at the register. The coffee is the best I've ever tasted, and the croissants are melt-in-your-mouth perfection. Michael and I shared one as we walked up and down the shop-lined streets admiring the window displays—a sex shop with romantic, lacy lingerie and strappy stiletto heels; a mystical bookstore advertising psychic readings and a large crystal collection; and a movie paraphernalia-shop window filled with Harry Potter wands, classic film posters, and a hanging model of a Star Wars TIE fighter.

Holding hands, we meandered along, sharing thoughts on a variety of topics with a keen interest in each other's ideas. It felt like our own private version of the movie *Before Sunrise*, the film directed by Richard Linklater in which an American man (Ethan Hawke) and a French woman (Julie Delpy) meet on a train, disembark in Vienna on a whim, and spend the night walking and talking, sharing their most intimate selves. The same thing often happens to Michael and me—long walks or drives tend to stimulate rich conversations through which we always seem to learn something new about each other.

At one point tears well up. *I've missed this,* I think to myself. *I need him with me, and it's time to make some tough decisions that will support our being together more. I need to rethink my work commitments and the travel they require*. And while that thought scares me when I consider what I may need to give up, the truth is my marriage is too important. As I get older, I'm realizing that in order to have the life I desire, one in which I'm more present and more peaceful, I need to resolve two needs that stand in opposition to each other. I love my work, and I enjoy teaching in different parts of the world, but I also need to be home more. I love interacting with readers and students, and yet I need time away from email and social media to focus on my personal life and my writing. I may need to accept that sometimes we must give up something we want in order to gain something we need.

At the end of the day, we joined Ileen for dinner at her favorite London restaurant. She invited her friend Karen to join us, and during the introductions Ileen happened to mention Michael's gift of psychic intuition and his ability to read people (with their permission). Intrigued, Karen asked Michael how it worked, and he offered his usual explanation: "I haven't a clue. I simply tune in to a person's energy, and I begin to get random thoughts and stories in my head that I say out loud."

I've seen Michael read people hundreds of times, and although the insights come to him in seemingly random bursts, in the end they make sense and are often remarkably accurate.

Although Michael has been intuitive from an early age, his ability to know things about people without knowing them personally went to a new level after he suffered through a four-year clinical depression. What started out as a bad reaction to medication descended into a long, dark night of the soul. But thanks to good doctors and a therapist who saw the spiritual crisis beneath the illness, Michael emerged from the darkness with a deeper understanding of himself, a genuine appreciation for the suffering of others, a sharpened gift of intuition—and the desire to use it. We never expected to see his depression as a gift, but it certainly turned out that way.

Over the last several years, in addition to his writing and working for his family business, Michael has provided private readings for individuals as well as group events to support local charities. He doesn't accept payment, which may be one reason why his impressions are so accurate; he has no attachment to being right. I remember a reading he did for Debbie Ford before she died. When she called and asked for his help, Michael identified specific things she was worrying about in relation to her business. He offered some possible solutions, and encouraged her to trust what she already knew to be true. He delivered such precise information that Debbie called me afterward and said, "I feel like he lifted off the top of my head and reached in and pulled out all the things that have been worrying me. Then he connected the dots, helped me to see things more clearly, suggested a course of action, and put the top back on!"

It's a bit surreal to watch Michael in action, although in this particular case, after Karen asked Michael to do a reading for her, Ileen and I did our best to give them privacy by talking to each other at the other end of the table. When they finished, Karen was deeply moved by the confirmation she received from Michael about two significant life changes that were already under way.

October 11th

This morning I'm missing home and Poupon. Michael and I are having such a terrific time here, and yet as the days go by, once again I feel like opposing forces are doing battle inside me. I'm doing my best to hold the tension of the opposites, but it's not easy. One side of me loves being in a new place, meeting new people, seeing new sights: she's the adventurer. The other longs for peace and the comforting routine of home life: she's the homebody. This internal tug-of-war usually begins around day three when I'm traveling alone, but because Michael is with me, it's taken a little longer to show up.

I feel so alone in my mental misery when this happens—as if I'm the only person on the planet who's ever felt this conflicted about being away from home. It's unsettling to be out to dinner with friends, enjoying a delicious meal and a great discussion, and suddenly be hit with a wave of melancholy that pulls me out of the present moment and up into my head. I start thinking about Poupon being without us for so long, and I slowly disappear from the conversation. I nod and smile as the ache in my chest starts to grow, and pretty soon I just want to get back to the hotel to be alone with my sadness. And it only gets worse when a harsh inner voice kicks in and starts judging these feelings. After all, I should be grateful for the chance to visit four exciting cities while someone is paying my way. Who am I to complain when I'm with colleagues and friends who take such good care of me? Most people would love a chance to visit Europe, so I should be enjoying myself instead of pining for home. Nothing like adding a little guilt to the misery.

I've been down this road before, and I've learned that the quickest way to relieve the pressure generated by my negative thinking is to talk about it, to give voice to the parts of me that are in dispute. Not always my first course of action, though. The role of lone ranger is a familiar one for me, a firstborn child with a legacy of sucking it up and dealing with difficult feelings on my own. But I know better now. Isolation just makes things worse. I end up twisting myself into an anxious mess, and the stress only escalates. I need to let Michael in on what's happening so he can bring a little sanity to the situation.

I stared out the window waiting for Michael to wake up and then told him about some of the internal chatter I've been listening to all morning. It turns out he has similar feelings. He loves the stimulation of the city, the visual feast and the chance to be with smart, interesting people. But he'd like to have more of these experiences closer to home. Michael's also missing Poupon, as well as his daily routine, and he's looking forward to being back. "But," he tells me, "it's pointless to focus on the upsetting feelings while we're still here, so I just put those thoughts aside as best I can." At moments like this I wish I could run a cord from his brain to mine and siphon off some of his enviable capacity for compartmentalization.

All in all, this trip is making me realize something important. It's time to get more of my need for connection and stimulation met in my personal life rather than just through my work. I've spent years traveling with a posse of colleagues who have become an on-the-road family, and I need to invest more energy in relationships at home. It's not easy, though, because when I return from a trip I spend so much time playing catch-up. There are to-do lists to complete, emails to respond to, and the need to handle all the daily responsibilities that come with running a home and a business. It's difficult to carve out the consistent time and space needed to cultivate intimate relationships.

Okay, too much thinking. It makes life feel like a never-ending battle, and I'm tired.

I want to live life, not conquer it.

Yes, change is on the horizon. Michael and I have spent the last twenty years working hard to pay off debt, save money, and get to the point where we can afford to enjoy more space and freedom in our lives; now we need to take advantage of it. I have limited time on the planet, and I want to use it in ways that bring me more joy and pleasure. It's so easy to get swept up in a successful career while losing sight of what I teach in the larger context of my life—the self-care message I wanted to remember after my interview in Germany. Each stage of life invites us to revisit our priorities, and I'm becoming more and more aware of a voice inside that won't be silenced, one that speaks to a different life my soul longs to experience. I'm hungry for depth, for space, and for being challenged in new ways. I need to listen to and act on that voice.

Right now I have to start working on the introduction for Debbie Ford's paperback release of *Courage*. I made a commitment to her editor to have it to him by early November, and I haven't even begun.

The irony of that last paragraph is not lost on me.

Later

Ileen's new movie, *Romeo & Juliet*, opens in the UK tonight, and I'm excited and nervous. It's been a long time coming. Michael and I attended the premiere in the US with her in late September, and it was the perfect exclamation point to her visit. Ileen invited me into her world of moviemaking when she took on this project three years ago. She allowed me to shadow her as she went through the process of bringing a major theatrical movie to the big screen, and I've been blessed with an inside view ever since. I've read several iterations of the script; watched early audition videos from the actors; learned about production budgets; watched dailies via the Web during actual shooting; and discussed with Ileen the deal-making, publicity, and marketing plans. She's given me complete access to a master's level program in filmmaking, and I've loved every single minute.

Working on the movie has been a fascinating experience that has awakened creative impulses that feel both exciting and scary. I love the idea of collaborating with a team of artists. Writing, by contrast, is such a solitary affair. I also love the thought of using a new medium to tell a story that will impact an audience. As I've gone through this moviemaking process with Ileen, I've noticed my soul saying, *Yes! Let's explore this world; let's stretch new muscles, learn something different.* But then my head joins the party. *Don't get too excited,* a cautionary voice tells me. *It's too late in life to think about doing something fanciful and so completely out of your lane.*

That sensible voice may have kept me safe over the years, but I'm beginning to realize it may also be strangling the life out of me. The truth is, being involved with the movie has put me in touch with things I love: period films; the beauty of set design, costumes, and architecture; fine acting; creative collaboration; and visual storytelling.

A door has been opened and I'm not sure I can shut it, although some part of me clearly thinks I should. The familiar can be so painfully safe. And while my subconscious mind may be masterful at coming up with reasons why I can't or shouldn't try something new, I'm too self-aware to be comfortable with maintaining the status quo.

I intend to keep my foot in that door.

In other news, I'm officially ready for home. Although I still have two more speeches to go, our trip has already been more than I hoped it would be—long walks, shopping for gifts, dinners with good friends, and several successful events. Now I need the restorative beauty of nature and the familiar routine of our home life. Robin tells me the leaves on the maple trees lining the driveway are just starting to change, and it feels good to know I'll be present for the turning of the seasons. I'm eager to watch the unfolding art show as it appears outside our windows every day.

The views; the surprise visits from animals and birds; the connection to life itself as the seasons birth new growth, thrive, and then give way to what's next, are becoming more and more significant to me. My love of nature has taken a backseat to my busy travel schedule, and I've lost touch with how vital the natural world is to my health and well-being. I have a limited number of seasons left, and I want to experience each one as fully as I can.

While I may be longing for home, I still need to go about my daily life here in London. This morning it's a visit to the grocery store, followed by a trip to the hair salon for a blow dry and manicure so I look presentable onstage. I fly to Salzburg first thing tomorrow to speak at another conference later in the day, and then back to London the following afternoon for a final presentation. The stress of preparing speeches for each venue, then delivering them to an international audience, is tough enough. But then add to that wardrobe changes, media interviews, business meetings, and the pressure of making flights on time in between countries, and it gets to be too much. And now Austria and London back-to-back in one weekend! This is c-r-a-z-y.

October 13th

What a trip! Yesterday I traveled to Salzburg to give my next talk. Michael stayed in London with Ileen, and I went with Robert, who was also speaking at the conference. As we flew over the Alps, I took out my iPhone and snapped a few pictures of the snow-covered mountaintops peeking through scattered clouds. The ethereal sight instantly connected me to something far greater than my small self, and a kind of spiritual contentment set in. Being eight miles high, plowing through the sky in a jet-propelled aluminum tube controlled by someone else, forces the ego into retreat. The vast universe below offers me a higher perspective, and I have a moment of clarity. The soul is here to experience life. Beauty, presence, and a connection to something greater than myself need to matter more than my ambition.

I arrived in Austria and gave my speech to a more subdued crowd than I'm used to. It's unsettling when I say something I think is funny and no one laughs. Or when I tell a touching story only to be met with blank stares. In that moment, the audience can only see an adult woman onstage wearing a dress and heels, but there's a cowering ten-year-old inside me wondering how the hell we wound up in front of so many people, and what we're going to do now that they don't seem to like us. When I'm onstage speaking, I need to be present, yet when I allow myself to be affected by the audience's reactions, I lose my connection. *They don't get you*, the little girl in my mind whispers. *They think you're boring and strange.*

It has taken years of practice and internal training, but now I know how to calm that little girl down while simultaneously addressing the audience. I put my hand on my heart, the signal for her to relax, then make eye contact with someone in the front row and speak directly to them. Once I feel the connection, and I almost always do when I look into someone's eyes, my inner girl relaxes and I'm able to reengage with the audience. I learned long ago that the quickest way to overcome anxiety about public speaking, regardless of where I am, is to take the focus off me and put it back where it belongs: on serving the needs of the people who have come to hear what I have to say.

After speaking and signing books into the afternoon, I went back to the hotel to join my colleagues and hosts for dinner. I had every intention of going to bed early, but was waylaid by familiar faces in the hotel lobby, colleagues I hadn't seen in a while. It was after midnight before I finished packing and got into bed, and 7 a.m. came quickly. Robert and I had a two-hour car ride to Munich to catch a direct flight to London so I could speak that afternoon. If not for the spectacular landscape and Robert's good company, I would have been miserable; cars on the autobahn drive much too fast for me. As our driver maintained speeds in excess of 160 kilometers per hour (almost 100 mph), I directed my attention to Robert, and to the snow-capped hills, lush countryside, and silvery mist hanging like translucent drapes over the land.

The flight to London was quick and easy, but we ran into heavy traffic between the airport and the hotel. I arrived at 2:00, took a quick shower, and dressed in a rush to make a 2:45 sound check. Twenty minutes to shower and get stage ready is too close for comfort. Rushing is not good self-care. Being a sensitive woman means I need to feel centered and grounded before getting onstage. Driving over in the car, I closed my eyes and took several slow, deep breaths, trying my best to pull my energy back into my body. *Something has to change*, a little voice inside me whispered once again. *I'm not sure I can operate at this pace anymore.*

That thought makes me nervous.

The good news is my presentation was well received by a warm and enthusiastic London audience. I always feel a special kind of connection to the people here. They smile, they laugh, they move in close. During my book signing afterward, I enjoyed meeting new friends and listening to their stories. Book signings allow for intimate moments with people who resonate with my work. For me they're sacred events. These are the people I hold in my heart and mind as I write.

Off to bed. Soon we head for home!

October 16th

I've just awakened from a long night's sleep to find the maple tree outside my bedroom window pulsating with light. From the horizon, a fiery sun ignites branches reaching toward my window. What a show! For as long as I can remember, I've had a love affair with light. I crave sunny days. As I work, I shuttle from room to room in search of sunbeams to sit in. Moonlight holds the same attraction.

Lying here with Poupon by my side, I stretch and smile at no one, feeling a wave of relief wash over me. It's good to be home. While our trip was wonderful in so many ways, I'm ready for time to myself, and for the comfort of my own bed. I look forward to sitting out on the back deck wrapped in a soft blanket, staring off into space as my cells drink in the vivid colors of a New England fall. No wonder I feared not getting home in time to catch this autumn show. As I sit here in bed staring out at the luminous maple, I'm filled with such gratitude for the little piece of heaven Michael and I have created for ourselves here. The barren branches of winter will most certainly have their own beauty. I'm just not ready for that yet.

The trip home was a long one that began with a familiar drill. Pack up the hotel room. Separate dirty clothes from clean. Fold and roll items so everything fits neatly in the suitcases. Go through drawers and closets twice to be sure nothing gets left behind. Run through the last-minute checklist to ensure we have what we need. Passports. Money. Itinerary. Even though my mind was barely engaged, I felt a new level of fatigue land in my body.

Thanks to the time change, we arrived home in the early afternoon, and the ritual began in reverse. Unpack clothes. Throw in a load of wash. Visit the Natural Grocer to get healthy food. Make green juice. Go for a long walk. It's interesting to note that as I engage in these tasks once home, I feel energized rather than fatigued. I actually get energy from cleaning up, creating order, and stocking the fridge. These rituals are like little anchors that fasten me to my life here, the comforting routines that welcome me back to the place my soul needs most right now.

By 9 p.m. I was spent, and fell into bed hoping for a good night's sleep. No sooner did I curl up and begin to drift off than Poupon joined me. Unlike some cats who ignore their owners when they return home from a trip, this little guy attaches himself to my hip.

I still remember the day we found Poupon, a tiny, blue-eyed ball of gray fur, at a local no-kill shelter. Someone had dropped him off that morning, and he was only a few weeks old. We showed up at the shelter after months of my begging Michael to consider bringing a cat into our home. More familiar with dogs, Michael was also in the throes of depression at the time, which meant he had no interest in adding more responsibility to our already overburdened lives.

But I was desperate for some kind of brightness. I'd grown weary of the perpetually overcast days that accompany depression, and I pleaded with Michael to at least consider the idea of adopting a cat. He finally gave in and agreed to visit a local shelter. As we walked around the room filled with kittens, a young man handed me this tiny boy, and I held him like a fine piece of china. When he started to purr, I handed him to Michael and watched as this fuzzy wizard cast a spell that claimed Michael's heart before his head had a chance to intervene.

We'd found our bright light.

We couldn't wait to bring our kitten home, and once it was safe to do so, we set up his temporary residence in the downstairs bathroom. We placed a small litter box next to the toilet and put a mini scratching post on the other side of the room. We added a soft, furry bed to the bathtub and threw in balls that squeaked like mice and other cat toys. For a time the three of us practically lived in that room. Playtime and training sessions merged into one as we swung feather-tipped fishing rods left and right and laughed for hours as Poupon bounced up and down on the floor. We marveled at how quickly he learned to use his scratching post once we strategically spread treats along its top edge. Before we knew it, Poupon turned into a timeless two-year-old, a sleek little jaguar with a plush silver coat.

In retrospect I see the perfection of a divine plan. We didn't rescue Poupon from the shelter that day. He rescued us.

As I sit here looking down at him cuddled in my lap, I remember a dream.

I'm back at a place I've been many times before—a beach, like Horseneck in Westport, MA. I'm with my sister Kerri and other people, and the views are beautiful. I'm staying at an old inn run by two men. I walk outside to the beach and find gorgeous light illuminating the ocean before me, roiled by huge waves. It's just before sunrise and I yell to Kerri, who comes out to have a look, and we are both stunned into silence by the beauty. I run back to get my camera to capture the light, but by the time I return the sun has risen and the moment is gone. We watch as the size of the waves increases, and as I move back from the encroaching tide, I suddenly step into a new dream.

I own a small shop that I'm redecorating. It's in another country, perhaps France. There's a woman who's helping me to clean windows in an inner room. They need to be cleaned one at a time, and only when the light is just right. She is silent, but her energy feels loving and helpful. Here at the shop I have a sense that something new is coming and I must get ready. When I step outside and walk down the street, I end up back at the ocean in the first dream. This time I feel more mature, stronger, and ready for what lies ahead. Then I wake up.

The first part of the dream brings me back to a special time in my life when I shared a beach house with a group of friends in my late twenties. I was unattached and had saved enough money to enjoy a month of freedom. I loved living by the ocean, where I could swim and bodysurf and run on the beach at sunset nearly every day. I marveled at the beauty that presented itself as only the sea can do. This part of the dream captures the feeling of that time—carefree, lighthearted, and happy.

It's what I long for now.

The second part of the dream is more mysterious, but it seems to reference the preparations necessary for this kind of change. I feel the need to make space, to refine my priorities, and to create a home that reflects the beauty and peace my soul desires. The slow, methodical cleaning of windows, and the support I receive for that task, is interesting. Am I trying to see something more clearly? What kind of help might I need to do so? And from whom?

There was a time in my life when dream work was a priority. I kept a journal specifically to record my dreams, and I paid close attention to the images and characters that showed up, knowing they were messengers bearing treasure from my unconscious mind. My psyche knew I was listening to myself in a deep and meaningful way, and as though it were casting bread crumbs on a trail, it led me to the places that needed attention and healing. It's doing that again now. The elements in these dreams—light, water, connection (to both my sister and the woman), a feeling of spaciousness, beauty, and the desire for clarity and simplicity—are all expressions of what my soul wants at this time in my life.

October 17th

I'm getting back into the swing of things today after the long trip, but I still feel so tired. My body wants to rest, but my mind keeps providing me with a running list of all the things I have to do. It has always been difficult for me to take a break when I feel a lull in my energy. I'm so used to pushing through a dip, but today I allowed myself to be guided by a wiser woman. I decided to curl up on the sofa and watch an episode of *The Good Wife*—a favorite indulgence thanks to Debbie, who turned me on to the show after the first season.

Within minutes, Poupon joined me. He jumped up on my lap, started kneading my stomach, and nestled into the crook of my arm the way he does when I've been gone for a long time. I turned off the TV, snuggled him close, and the next thing I knew he woke me by twitching during his own dream. I stood and stretched, feeling that delicious sense of restored peace that an afternoon nap can sometimes deliver.

It's a sign of progress that I listened to the wise woman instead of the taskmaster. Little changes make for bigger transformations. One small step at a time is what will allow me to reclaim a better sense of balance.

October 18th

This morning I woke to what sounded like gunfire. I must check to see if hunting season has started. I respect that some people need to hunt for food, but knowing and loving deer as I do, I cannot imagine any human being looking at a buck or a doe and pulling the trigger. It's an unexpected downside of moving to the country. I had no idea that I'd be forced to wrestle with the heartbreak that consumes me when I hear gunshots in the distance. It's times like this when I wish I wasn't so sensitive. It's all I can do to shake off the despair and go about my day.

Last night I slept soundly, woke with the sunrise, and decided to read a bit of May Sarton's *Encore: A Journal of the Eightieth Year*. I'm ingesting it slowly, one page at a time, sometimes one paragraph at a time, because it's one of her last. I open the book at random and find a sentence written after her return home from a trip to London:

> There is a slight lifting of the air so I can smell the earth for the first time, and yesterday I took possession of my life here.

Unpacking, doing laundry, cleaning the cat box, playing with Poupon, and working in the garden—these are activities that help me to take possession of my life here, too. These are the ways I mark my territory, to use Poupon as my muse. My professional life also beckons, including the ritual of going through the mail. There are bills to be paid, letters to read and respond to, and manuscripts with requests for endorsements. I have to be in the right state of mind to do this, as it can easily feel overwhelming.

After almost two weeks of travel, there's a whole tub from the post office—books, CDs, bills, magazines, and catalogs. I've learned to be ruthless, quickly weeding out everything that's nonessential and piling it up for the recycling bin. *When in doubt, throw it out.* Once the mail is sorted, I prepare to pay bills. Over the years, with Michael's help, I've trained myself to see this activity as an abundance ritual.

In my late twenties, when I struggled to make ends meet, the folder that contained my bills was a source of anxiety. As I paid them I saw the amount in my checking account dwindle, and I never felt like there was enough. Finally, fed up with suffering, I took on my financial health as a serious project and got an extra job. I created a plan to eliminate my debt, and over the course of a year I used the extra money to pay off my credit cards once and for all. Then I trained myself to keep the balances small enough so they could be paid in full at the end of the month.

I'm grateful that throughout our marriage, Michael has shared my desire to live debt-free and well within our means. That said, he's always been more comfortable spending money, and as both our incomes increased, he helped me to see that hiring people to do the things we no longer wanted to do and making purchases that enhanced our life were simply a way of circulating the energy of abundance. This new belief inspired me to create a ritual of gratitude and celebration when paying our bills, and I've done so ever since.

Today I gathered my supplies: a pile of cards with beautiful art and positive messages, colorful stickers, and my favorite stamps. I like mixing beauty, creativity, and an element of surprise because it makes bill-paying fun. After writing checks and putting them in envelopes, I place a card from one of my decks in with the check and then use postage stamps with images of hearts or animals. I love the idea of sending one of my grace cards to the IRS, or a self-care card to our insurance company. Recently I discovered that the man who mows our lawn saves the cards I send him, and it makes me smile to think of the collection hanging on the wall in his office.

I've used this ritual for a long time now, and it has turned what used to be a stressful task into an empowering experience. I have no doubt that the abundance that has come into my life is a direct result of the change in my attitude about money and paying bills. Being grateful as we pay for what we've received invites even more to be grateful for.

Now that the mail and bills are handled, I'm off for an afternoon walk with my sister Kerri.

October 19th

This morning I lie in bed working on a newsletter in my head. As I sift through the past week, revisiting events in my life, I wait for thoughts to arrange themselves into a narrative that catches my attention. Actually, it needs to catch my heart. I love it when an experience or idea grabs me emotionally because I know that I'll be fully engaged, and chances are the reader will be, too. Then I start to rearrange these thoughts into some kind of ordered life lesson.

So much of writing occurs in my mind while I'm doing other things. I've trained myself to observe life, and to see the metaphors that provide a new perspective or helpful lesson. The removal of dead tree branches in the yard, which provides greater access to sunlight, mirrors my need to cut away whatever I no longer love or need in my life so I can feel lighter and more open to new growth. Or the obsessive fear of how a home repair may turn out to be extensive or expensive *before* the problem has even been assessed reminds me to stop expecting problems in other areas of my life, too.

This morning I decide to write about my reaction to a story I heard on NPR yesterday. It was about a woman named Zora who, from the time she was five years old, had a recurring dream of becoming a superhero. This dream inspired Zora to make a list of all the skills she would need to master in order to achieve this goal—martial arts, evasive driving, knife throwing, defusing bombs—so she could then develop each one. On hearing her list of accomplishments, which included graduating from high school at fifteen, finishing a bachelor's degree at eighteen and a master's at twenty, and completing the course work for a Ph.D. in geopolitics by twenty-one, I felt like such an underachiever.

Now if I were to die tomorrow, I'd certainly leave feeling at peace with what I've accomplished, but all I could think about was that I hadn't learned to do nearly as much over my entire lifetime as Zora had accomplished by age twenty-one! Not to mention that I don't have a college degree. As soon as that thought crossed my mind, I stopped the crazy train in its tracks. For years I've compared myself to others. I've held up my accomplishments next to the achievements of my peers. I've measured my attractiveness against the outfit of another woman. Or I've judged the success of a book (or the lack thereof) against the success of books written by colleagues or friends. When playing this silly game, I rarely measure up. And worse, a militant part of me attempts to use this practice as motivation, pushing me to perform, reach higher, do more, be better, blah, blah, blah, blah, blah. Of course it never works. I've never been motivated to do more by feeling less than. I've never been inspired to reach higher by putting myself in the one-down position. I've never ever done my best after berating myself for not being good enough.

I'm grateful that I've finally developed the habit of catching myself when I start playing the comparison game. I've learned to use it as a trigger to focus on what I do have, on what I'm grateful for, and on the assets that make me unique and special. That's good self-care.

After hearing Zora's story and shifting my perspective, I realized that by being more loving to myself and modeling it for others, I have a chance to be a different kind of superhero: a woman who reflects self-acceptance and compassion in a way that can extend out to every person I meet.

Now there's the story I need to use for my blog post!

October 21st

Like the lilacs and peonies that pay an oh-too-brief visit in spring, the autumn colors are changing too quickly this year. The weather has been so dry that the leaves are turning faster than usual. The sugar maples in the front yard have gone from yellow to orange to red in just a few days. A few days!

I want to yell,

Stop!

Wait!

Not yet!

My psyche needs time to make the transition.

The more I value that which tugs at my heart—nature and the beauty of the changing seasons, things that feed a growing hunger—the more crucial they become. Autumn is a time of surrender, a slow release into the reality of death, but I don't want to surrender sooner than I must. The fading light, the cool breeze that brings a chilling hint of winter, and the geese flying overhead at the start of their migration force me to face the fact, once again, that everything ends.

Endings. It's *the* theme this year. I seem to be entering a stage of life where I feel compelled to stop for a while and reflect. I need a long, deep breath. Space to digest my life thus far. I want to search my history for wisdom and for those things I value most so I can keep them front and center. I know that's why I feel so drawn to nature—the place that hosts my curiosity. As a kid I spent hours sitting under trees, staring at clouds or at birds in flight. I'd get lost in the woods looking for insects and wildflowers and snakes. The outside world was a magical place, full of life, always presenting something new to marvel at—baby birds in a nest, the forsythias planted by my grandfather, their yellow arms reaching this way and that, or the green shoots that materialized in just a few days after planting a garden. The outdoors was my home away from home, a place to find myself, free from the noise of a big family.

Today, nature rescues me from a different kind of noise. The busyness of my life. The worry that accompanies ambition. The endless thoughts about all that must be done. As I walk along the reservoir, hike through the state park near our home, ride waves in the heat of the summer, or simply stare out over the fields in our backyard, I feel transported, reconnected to something ancient and true. I can count on the trees and the wind and the water to remind me of what matters most to my soul.

Yes, that little girl was on to something. I'm ready to come home again.

October 22nd

Yesterday Ashley came to visit with her son, Greyson, who's eleven. Ashley was the literary agent both Michael and I worked with when we were writing our first books, before she left publishing to master real estate, interior design, and graphic art. Ashley is our kind of girl—quirky, curious, smart, and ever so generous of spirit. She's a modern-day flower child with a Texan twist. When she arrived, I opened the front door to find her standing there in a tie-dyed shirt, bell-bottom jeans, and well-worn cowboy boots. "Hi, y'all!" she hollered, a wide smile splashed across her face. I grabbed her, gave her a bear hug, and ushered her into the house.

Ashley and her husband, Grant, are homeschooling Greyson, and she's taking him on an East Coast trip to visit friends, museums, and historical sites, so they came to stay with us overnight. For dinner Michael and I took them to Woodman's, the place where fried clams were invented, for a true New England clambake. We had lobsters, clams, corn on the cob, and plenty of lively conversation. Back home afterward, Greyson taught me how to use a new app called Vine to record six-second videos and edit them any way I like. Greyson downloaded the app, set up my account, and showed me how to film and edit mini movies in less than five minutes. We roared with laughter as we recorded ourselves making funny faces and goofy noises. Even Poupon got into the act—we filmed him as he swaggered down the hallway, full of disdain for our noisy charades.

Today we went to the small cemetery of Newbury's first settlers, whose graves date back to the 1600s, and we continued our filming. It's amazing how much you can fit into a six-second video. We recorded snapshots of old gravestones, as well as of Greyson walking like a mummy and then jumping out from under a pile of leaves. We also visited the alpacas near Little's Farm, had brunch at Angie's diner downtown, and drove out to the beach for a long walk. There were people with dogs running all over the place, and it gave Ashley and Greyson a chance to get a furry fix. Like me, they love all kinds of animals and have quite the paradise back home—a farm with chickens, pigs, dogs, cats, and ducks on ten acres of land outside of Austin, Texas. My idea of heaven. Sort of. I can't imagine the work it takes to maintain the place!

Ashley and Greyson left before sunset, and we said our sad goodbyes with promises of another visit. I miss them already. Their energy and enthusiasm for life is contagious, and they leave me wanting more . . .

Tonight while on the treadmill, I glanced out at the back-yard and paused my workout, feeling complete awe as the setting sun bathed the line of trees going down to the reservoir in a soft, amber light. Nearly every day I thank God for the breathtaking beauty here in our little carved-out corner of the world.

October 23rd

It's 9 a.m., and I can't believe I slept this late. Michael must have fed Poupon, or he would be walking all over my head trying to get me to fill his bowl by now. I don't know how cat owners get sufficient sleep—ever.

I go downstairs, and as I open the door to the deck, I feel the brush of crisp air against my skin and decide to throw on a coat and go out for a long walk. I have so much to do in my office, but these days I'm giving those tasks secondary importance. It's as if the personality that has operated as Cheryl Richardson for most of my life has been hijacked by a new version, leaving me unable to perform old functions. I watch myself saying no in order to do more of the things that matter to my soul, and while I feel guilty, I'm still not willing to change what I'm doing.

I'd say that's called growth.

October 25th

Another stellar day. It's getting cold, though. I woke this morning with Poupon snuggled under my arm, his little head hidden beneath his paws—another sign that the seasons are changing. Staring at his sweet face while he sleeps, I'm aware, once again, that I'm trying to straddle two worlds, one in which I travel and teach and another in which I rest and tend the garden of my creative impulses. It's difficult to be spontaneous or to honor my needs when I have to fulfill earlier commitments booked more than a year in advance. I'm trained to put my head down and soldier on, but now that I'm in menopause, I don't have the tolerance I used to have, and it's getting harder to do. I need to find a way to make it work.

I'm off to New York this weekend for my final public event with Louise Hay. She's made the decision to retire and come off the road, and it's bittersweet for me. I'm excited by the prospect of seeing her and celebrating together, but I also have to make amends with the part of me that feels the tug of home, hearth, and hibernation.

This morning, as I made tea and fed Poupon, I pulled out a small jar of lavender honey given to me by a gentleman in Hamburg, Germany. Having read a Facebook post I wrote about appreciating the multiple kinds of honey served with tea while in his country, he left a gift for me with someone who stood in my book-signing line. When I got to my room later that day and opened it up, I found five jars of honey—most of which had names I couldn't decipher, except that one was lavender. As I wrapped them in paper to pack in my bag, I could feel the love that inspired his gift. People can be so incredibly kind.

What is it about honey? I wonder. I've rarely considered it in the past, but for some reason honey has become a thing for me this year. Just as a dream invites the unconscious mind to lay its gifts at our feet, a new object of affection can hold clues to what's brewing beneath the surface. So with that in mind, I want to explore what honey represents:

Bees

Nature

Cycles of life

The power of community

Native nourishment

Sweetness

Pleasure

As I look at this list, I'm stunned by how relevant these terms are to my life right now: my desire to just *be* for a while; my need to be around nature as a vital source of energy and joy, pondering the cycles of the seasons, and of life in general;

my longing to create a community of like-minded friends near home; and my new, emerging priority of pleasure. No wonder honey keeps showing up in my life. It's a messenger, a sweet reflection of what's becoming increasingly important to me now.

Today I notice a part of me settling into winter. My body had been so out of rhythm with all the traveling, and I just wasn't ready to say goodbye to fall. But as the nights get colder, I can feel myself slipping into acceptance. Time moves on. Now in my fifties, I'm trying to come to terms with the fact that I'm closer to the finish line than the starting gate. I find myself measuring time more by the seasons than by years. To say I'm at midlife sounds less urgent than to say I may have thirty or forty summers left. Snowshoeing around the reservoir in winter, walking the beach during a summer sunset, planting the garden in spring, and feasting on the abundance of autumn color, all give new meaning to the preciousness of time here. I want to be present for as many of these experiences as I can.

When we're young, we assume we'll live forever. Youth keeps the finish line at bay. Then a significant birthday comes along, or a New Year's celebration that marks the passing of another year, or a frightening experience like the need for a biopsy or the unexpected loss of a loved one, and we're suddenly forced to face the reality that our time here is so exquisitely limited.

October 26th

I'm on the train heading to NYC for the conference with Louise this weekend. At the last minute, Scott, my vocal coach, decided to join me on the trip, and we've been having fun talking about music and looking at photographs on his iPad. He's not only a gifted singing teacher, he's also a passionate photographer who travels the world taking pictures. As we marvel at an image of Machu Picchu in early light, Scott explains that he got to the entrance gate before sunrise and the onslaught of tourists to get the shot. Bathed in the first glimpse of daybreak, the ancient stone structures perched on the side of the mountain are shrouded in mist. The photo looks worthy of *National Geographic*.

Scott's a new addition to my life. Back in June I was enjoying dinner with a friend who's a professional singer, when she happened to mention finding a new vocal coach. "He's one of the best I've ever worked with," she said, "and he's close by. So if you ever need a singing teacher, I'll hook you up."

Little did she know that just that morning I'd been toying with the idea of taking singing lessons again.

My love of singing started in high school, fostered by the passion of my music teacher, Mr. Volpe. Mr. Volpe went beyond the basics to train us in advanced subjects like music theory, counterpoint, and solfège—a method for developing pitch and learning to sight read by singing notes on sheet music. I never learned to play an instrument, but practicing solfège awakened something inside me, and I became fascinated with writing music and using my voice. Over the years I've taken lessons now and then, attempting to reignite this love, but inevitably I'd end up feeling frustrated and give up. My last lesson was ten years ago, when I told myself that learning to sing wasn't a productive or reasonable use of my time. I had no plans to be singing onstage anytime soon.

Enter perimenopause.

The interests of my adolescent years came back with a vengeance as I headed toward menopause. Years ago, Christiane Northrup, an expert on women's health, said something to me that turned out to be a foreshadowing of things to come: "During perimenopause, you'll have a chance to revisit your adolescent years to heal and deal with anything that hasn't been dealt with yet, *and* you'll rediscover desires that may have been suppressed around the time of puberty."

I'm so grateful now for Chris's advance warning. When I look back in time, I notice that my adolescent interests bear a striking resemblance to the desires that are emerging now:

A longing for liberation

The hunger to express myself creatively

A rekindling of my love of music and singing

A deep feeling of loneliness, coupled with a desire to be left alone

The desire for true peers—friends with whom I share common ground emotionally, spiritually, and intellectually, and who challenge me to grow

A need to be in nature, exploring, planting gardens, watching flowers grow

A love of animals and birds

The need to surround myself with beauty

It seems that "the change" involves challenging the way I've lived my life up to this point—worshipping at the altar of efficiency, always striving and pushing to make things happen, and taking care of others at the expense of my own needs. These behaviors aren't working anymore, and finding new ones requires slowing down and honoring parts of me that have been ignored.

That night at dinner when my friend mentioned her new vocal coach, my soul bypassed my head and went straight to my mouth. "Yes, I'd love to have the name," I told her, pulling out a pen and piece of paper from my handbag.

"Scott Richardson," she replied.

I looked up, surprised that he and I shared the same last name. *Of course we do*, I thought to myself as I wrote down Scott's number, chuckling at the way the Universe had just confirmed my decision. I called him the next day.

When Scott and I first spoke, he sounded nice enough on the phone, even teasing me by calling me "Cuz." Not that his niceness mattered. He could have sounded like the most loving, compassionate, nonjudgmental person in the world, and I would have still felt like a swarm of butterflies had taken possession of my stomach. As much as I love to sing, doing so in front of others makes me self-conscious, and that's a feeling I prefer to avoid.

Nevertheless, remembering my desire to challenge my inhibitions, I took my terrified little kid by the hand, promised to keep her safe, and went to see Scott.

Scott teaches at his house, his golden retriever, Buck, by his side—and when we met he greeted me with a warm hug. I liked him instantly. As soon as we walked into his studio, I admitted I was afraid of singing in front of him. "Okay, sit down," he directed, as he pulled a worn black swivel chair over from its place in front of an electronic keyboard. "Look, I'm not here to judge you," Scott said with a mock sternness. "We're here to have fun. Got it?"

Fun. Now there's a word missing from my vocabulary, I thought to myself. I made a note to add it to my new list of emerging priorities.

Scott taught me goofy exercises designed to release the tightness in the muscles around the neck, the ones that needed to be relaxed in order to sing joyfully. *Another metaphor for life,* I thought, *the need to relax, to allow, to soften.* As he played scales on the piano, I followed along, singing the notes while rolling my tongue as if I were pronouncing *r*'s in Spanish. Scott then had me purse my lips like a kid making the sound of a motorboat as I continued to run through the scales. Within twenty minutes the tension subsided, and

I started to sing a few songs. By the end of the lesson, I knew two things: I'd found a great teacher, and singing for the sheer joy of it *was* a productive use of my time.

I booked four more lessons, took a CD Scott recorded with the exercises on it, and left promising to practice.

As I sit here on the train on my way to New York City, I think about the importance of relaxing the hypervigilant, overly responsible part of me that's always on the lookout for the next thing I have to do. It's time to take advantage of the financial foundation Michael and I have built over the last twenty years and enjoy life more. Desire keeps calling, and I need to answer.

October 28th

It was quite the whirlwind trip to New York City. The event with Louise was terrific. It gives me enormous pleasure to watch people interact with her. While I'm proud to have taught with a woman who is so influential in my field, what really makes me happy is knowing I've helped her get back in touch with her fans. When we first began speaking together, it had been twenty years since Louise had been onstage, and she was understandably nervous. So we worked out a plan. I'm good at creating a safe place onstage, and she's good at improvising.

So I'd draft the initial outline for our talks, get her feedback, and make adjustments. Then, once we were in front of the audience, I'd initiate a discussion between us that left her free to respond and improvise. Louise's timing is impeccable, and she has a terrific sense of humor, prompting unexpected one-liners that left the audience (and me!) in tears.

Sometimes I wonder if before we were born our souls made an agreement to work together at this particular point in our lives. I like to think so.

I'm glad Scott decided to come with me, and Michael, who couldn't join us, is happy I have company on this trip. Over lunch Scott suggested we take in a Broadway show—when I told him I'd never seen one, I thought he was going to fall over. "Are you kidding me?" he exclaimed. "You *really* haven't seen a Broadway show?" Nope, I told him, the closest I've come is seeing the Rockettes' *Christmas Spectacular* at Rockefeller Center years ago with Michael and our parents. "I'm ready," I tell Scott. "Let's do Broadway."

After standing in the Times Square TKTS line for two and a half hours, we finally got tickets for *The Book of Mormon* and ended up in the seventh row just off center stage. The set was incredible, the music and dancing beyond amazing, and the irreverence was completely unexpected. Although Scott gave me a bit of background on the show, neither one of us was prepared for how outrageous the story turned out to be. Scott was right. There's nothing like a Broadway show, and this one is sure to be the first of many. I look forward to sharing the experience with Michael sometime soon!

The next morning, I took my place onstage at the Javits Center for our own show. Perched on high stools with a table between us, Louise and I shared our favorite affirmations, funny stories from the road, and what we've learned from each other about loving ourselves while writing *You Can Create an Exceptional Life* together. At one point I looked over at Louise while she was talking to the audience and felt such appreciation for our time together. Never in a million years could I have imagined that life would have led me here.

When finished, Louise and I spent two hours signing books. I had made a decision to not do any photos (thanks to Michael's insistence), and it made all the difference. Being less distracted, I had much more energy for interacting with people. When lines are long, the time it takes to pose for photos means that people end up having to wait longer than they should. Not to mention that I feel cameras intrude on what should be an intimate, private moment.

Scott was a trouper, sitting nearby while I signed books, and when I finished we took off for his favorite camera store so he could look at lenses. I decided to take full advantage of being with an expert photographer. I'd wanted to get a digital camera, having outgrown the one in my iPhone, so I ended up getting myself a small Sony digital with a fantastic telephoto lens. Scott showed me how to use it, and now I'm off and running (or shooting)!

That was more excitement in such a short period than I've had in a long time. I'll sleep well tonight!

October 29th

I awoke from nine straight hours of sleep to a rising sun and a whining cat. Poupon rarely makes it past 7 a.m. before trying to get Michael or me to feed him. I slept in the guest bedroom last night so I could get the rest I needed. I can't get used to Michael's white-noise machine or the fan blowing cool air over our bed. We have such different sleep-hygiene needs that we may have to work out some kind of compromise. Sure enough, at seven sharp I could hear Poupon in the guest bathroom unraveling the toilet paper from the roll—his new trick. Before I went downstairs, I made sure I fixed the holder so it will be harder to unravel tomorrow morning. We'll see how long it takes our Mensa cat to figure out a way around it.

I love sleeping and especially like it when I sleep late. It hasn't always been that way, though. I used to be hard on myself when I didn't get up early. If I slept past eight I'd tell myself I was being lazy, and I'd start the day in a bad mood. But that's another thing that has changed as I've gotten older. After paying more attention to how I feel after a good night's rest—clear-headed, energetic, creative, and hopeful—I'm perfectly okay with staying in bed if that's what it takes. Good sleep is great self-care.

October 30th

I've had to give several interviews over the last two days. The first was with a writer from a magazine in London who wanted to talk about what it was like to be mentored by Louise Hay. She was excited about having the conversation, which always makes it easier, and I decided to use our interview as a chance to celebrate my work with Louise as our time together draws to a close.

I first met Louise when I picked her up at an airport more than twenty years ago. I had just embarked on my own journey of personal growth by volunteering to help out at one of her events. Fifteen years later, she welcomed me to an authors' party hosted by her company, Hay House. Since then we've written a book together and traveled the world to teach, and I've learned a great deal from this remarkable woman. Louise has taught me to pay close attention to what I think and say, to never forget that words possess tremendous power—her precision with language is a form of mastery.

Louise loves to catch me using words or phrases that miss the mark. If I say, "I can't wait to see you again," she'll flash an impish smile and say, "You mean, 'I'm looking forward to seeing you.'" Or if I say, "Don't forget that we're meeting downstairs at eight," she'll immediately respond with, "You mean, 'Please remember.'" While these might seem like insignificant examples of good-natured teasing, Louise's reminders have helped me to become far more aware of what I say both to myself and others.

Now when I hear myself complain about something, I realize right away that my negativity is affirming the very thing I don't want. When I make it a daily practice to take stock of what I'm grateful for, I can see how I'm putting creative energy behind what I want more of in my life. I still have the affirmation inspired by Louise, *I am showered with good thoughts all day long*, hanging on the glass wall of the shower at home, and I think of her every time I read it. Louise is a master at cultivating good thoughts.

My interview ran more than an hour, and at the end of it I felt good. My words clearly reflected my admiration for this amazing woman whose affirmative spirit launched an entire movement—one that has had a global impact on people's lives. I completed two more interviews after that, and that should do it for the winter.

Speaking of winter, this weekend we turn the clocks back, so the sun will be setting around 4 p.m. For years I've hated this time of year—the loss of light, the quickening days, the lack of easy movement here in the Northeast once the cold, snow, and ice set in. But then something shifted. While I was writing *The Art of Extreme Self-Care* back in 2008, I began to experience winter as the ideal time for me to draw my energy inward and enjoy a more contemplative life while I write.

Now I look forward to hibernating, keeping this journal, taking singing lessons, and decorating the house. I might even update my wardrobe with clothes that reflect more of who I am at this time in my life—something else I've wanted to do for a long time.

I have to say that Michael's introduction to bright light therapy has had a lot to do with changing my tune about winter. For years I struggled with seasonal affective disorder (SAD), a type of depression related to seasonal changes. Winter would set in, sunlight would grow scarce, and I'd start to feel both melancholy and ravenously hungry. I'd descend into carbohydrate hell in an unconscious attempt to boost my flagging energy, because exercise felt like an onerous chore. My lack of movement only made my mood worse. I dreaded winter until I met Michael, and he recognized what was going on. "You need bright light therapy," he said one afternoon, and then suggested that we head to the store to buy me a light box. Within days I noticed a difference. My mood improved, I had energy and felt like moving my body, and I was better able to regulate what I ate. I've kept a light box close at hand ever since.

October 31st

Boo! Today Halloween welcomed me with a "moment of amazement," as poet Mary Oliver might say. As I lay in bed, slowly coming to life, I looked up just in time to see a fog bank float in front of the maple tree outside the bedroom window. One minute the tree was there, and the next it vanished, as if with a wave of a magician's hand.

Yesterday I drove to Portsmouth to see Scott for a singing lesson. In order to not feel anxious on my way there, I distracted myself with as many goofy vocal exercises as I could remember. Then, when I got to the lesson, I spent nearly the entire hour doing my best to overcome my self-consciousness. Today my assistant, Nicole, asked if the hardest part of the lesson was learning breath control, to which I replied, absolutely not. The hardest part is learning to relax, have fun, and let go of the need to sound good.

This week we're working on Bonnie Raitt's version of the John Prine song "Angel from Montgomery." Scott insists that he and I will perform it together at an open-mike night at some point, and I humor him with a noncommittal smile. I'm pretty sure that's not going to happen, although I confess that despite my jitters driving to the lesson, by the time I leave I'm giddy with delight. I'm having fun for the sake of it. Yes, I'm also learning and developing a new skill, but I like that it's my secret pleasure, one that doesn't get shared with the world.

November 1st

On a train to NYC once again! I got up early, made green juice, and then did something I've never done before. I packed a *big* bag for a three-day trip. Usually I'm a master of travel efficiency, but this time, in honor of Debbie Ford, who loved to take lots of clothes with her whenever she traveled, I decided to give myself options. Thank goodness for redcaps and doormen who stand ready to help a woman in need.

Later

Tonight Reid Tracy, the president of Hay House, and I began teaching our *Speak, Write & Promote* workshop at the Hotel Pennsylvania. We're staying at another venue—a small, contemporary place in Hell's Kitchen, but decided to hold our program here, across from Penn Station, to make it easier for out-of-town travelers. While there are hints of classic elegance in our ballroom, the place has certainly seen better days. It's dark and dreary and could use a good cleaning. As I walked onstage to set up my computer, I looked around the room and made a mental note to let the event director know that we ought to upgrade the venue for future seminars. I'm learning to value my need for beauty. While I don't want to appear high maintenance, the truth is that a clean, pleasing environment is a vital source of energy that allows me to do my best work. And it's good for those attending as well. Fortunately the Hay House event team gets it, and I know they'll understand.

In this program, we walk attendees through the most effective way to use writing, speaking, and media to build a larger audience for their work. Between the two of us, Reid and I have years of experience to share, and we always have a good time teaching together. Reid has turned Louise Hay's successful company into the largest self-help publisher in the world, harnessing the power of the Internet in ways most publishers are still trying to get a handle on. He's also great at producing and marketing online courses, and he knows the publishing world inside and out. Reid played a significant role in shaping the careers of many high-profile authors like Suze Orman, Iyanla Vanzant, and Dr. Wayne Dyer. His savvy and my experience as an entrepreneurial author—who has published several best-selling books, built a lucrative speaking career, and used the Internet to create a following of loyal readers—offer our attendees a solid road map to success. And they're excited to take the journey.

When the event begins, I look out over the audience and take in the hopeful, anxious-looking faces. I know that most of these people, while eager to get started, will be surprised by what's required to become a successful author and lecturer. Long days of pounding the pavement (or working the phone), connecting with people, and looking for opportunities to share your work. Delivering scores of free speeches before you ever get paid for one. Writing endless "shitty first drafts," as Anne Lamott puts it, for blogs, newsletters, and books, until you find your voice and connect with your audience. Giving hundreds of interviews with energy and enthusiasm, even when a host is clearly pressed for time or not really interested in what you have to say.

And then there's the inner work. Learning to quiet the ego when faced with tough editorial feedback, negative reviews, or the public criticism of your work. Or cultivating the patience and tenacity needed to hang in there through the inevitable disappointments and failures. And there will be plenty.

The first night went well, and we have a great group of people on board. Now it's time for a good night's sleep, but I need to call Michael first. He waits patiently for me to touch base at the end of each day when I travel, and I like to make sure I have enough energy left for a coherent conversation. Sometimes it's hard, though, because I'm so tired. Holding the projections and expectations of an audience takes a tremendous amount of energy. Not to mention the fact that I spend hours talking when I'm teaching a weekend workshop. What I really need by the end of the day is to shut my mouth and crawl under the covers. But our marriage is important to me, and it needs nurturing, especially while I'm on the road.

November 3rd

I love a big sky view. My hotel room is on the ninth floor overlooking the Hudson River, with cruise ships as big as cities docked at the piers below. I'm grateful for this wide lens; it makes being in a hotel more comfortable. As I sit here waiting for breakfast, I feel an old, familiar sadness creeping in. I miss Michael and Poupon. It's been two days, but it already feels like a week, and I still have two more to go. Hotel life is lonely, and while I know I'll miss teaching now that I'm headed home for a break, I look forward to getting back to the routines that bring order and peace to my life.

November 4th

This morning the sun is rising on the Hudson River, drenching the trees in pale gold. The bed is positioned in a way that allows me to wake to a full view of the river, and it's gorgeous. It's cold in my hotel room, though. I shut the heat off last night before I went to bed because I couldn't stand the noise or the forced hot air blowing on me, and I just discovered that it's thirty-three degrees outside. It looks cold.

Soon I'll be going home to winter. Time to tussle with the melancholy moments that arise as I prepare for limited access to the outside world. For now, though, I'm going to enjoy my last hotel breakfast on the road while curled up in bed appreciating this view.

November 6th

For some reason, I've felt unusually sensitive today, as if my protective outer layer has suddenly become paper thin. Debbie has been on my mind again. Tonight in the bath, I stared at the statue of a Balinese goddess that's sitting on the shelf next to the tub, a gift she gave me on the last day we were together. My mind wandered back to our visit, and I felt struck by a cannonball of grief.

My connection with Debbie was unique. We spoke the same language; shared a profession as coaches, writers, and teachers; and were both deeply committed to our own growth—and to each other's. Debbie and I could talk shop, counsel each other, and giggle together about the peaks and pitfalls of living on the road in airplanes and hotels. She understood my world as no one else could. I had expected to enjoy our friendship for a lifetime, but it culminated in our painful goodbye in February of 2013.

I'll be forever grateful for the major snowstorm that provided me the chance to see Debbie one last time before she died. I was finishing up a retreat I'd been leading in Tucson, Arizona, when we heard that airports in the northeast corridor were closing due to snow. According to the news, it could be days before they opened, and my travel agent was already looking for future flights and alternative routes home. At lunch a friend mentioned that she was driving six hours through the desert to San Diego, where Debbie lived. Walking down the path to my room afterward, something told me to go back to the dining room, find my friend, and ask if there was space in her car. "Of course," Kristina said, "we'd love for you to join us!" Back at my room, I sent up a silent prayer of thanks and packed my bags.

When I got to Debbie's building, the elevator ride to her apartment felt endless. I had called ahead to say that I was coming, and I was told that death was close. I wasn't sure I was ready for the emotional impact of seeing its advance firsthand. When I entered Debbie's room and carefully sat down next to her on the bed, my eyes were drawn to the pink nail polish on her fingers, its brightness such a stark contrast to the translucent skin. We smiled at each other as I pulled her hands into mine. I noticed she wore the same faded red string around her wrist that I wore—part of a blessing ritual we shared just a few months earlier after Debbie returned from Israel. As she closed her eyes to rest for a while, I slipped my phone out of my pocket and snapped a picture of our hands clasped together.

Now and then Debbie would open her eyes and speak, her faint voice straining against the effort. "Cheryl," she whispered, "I love you, so please, *please*, don't waste your time doing things you don't really want to do. Right now it doesn't matter how many best-selling books I've written, or how many fans I have on Facebook. All I care about is leaving my son and the people I love behind, and what will happen after I die." She smiled weakly, but her gaze was fierce. My eyes filled with tears. I felt wobbly, barely able to keep it together. "And for God's sake, don't do anything that bores you."

Her words struck me with particular force. Because we led such similar lives, it felt like Debbie was giving me my own deathbed perspective. And the timing couldn't have been better. Here I was beginning to question everything, craving more depth in my work and in my relationships, feeling a growing need for new creative expression, and Debbie was pushing me to take these desires seriously.

I sat holding her hands for more than an hour as she slept, her breathing labored and shallow. I tried to memorize the shape of her mouth, the arch of her beautiful brows, the lines on her delicate, graceful hands. When it came time to leave, I gently kissed her forehead and promised to stay in touch via her assistant, Julie, a benevolent soul who had been by her side nonstop for days. As I crawled into the backseat of the car that picked me up, I stared out the window, feeling gutted and disturbed. *How do I live the same life after this?*

That day affected me in ways I still don't fully understand. As painful as it is to lose someone we love, there's also a gift to be had. Death opens a window, and for a brief time our priorities come into view. We know who and what matters most, and we're brave enough to ignore the rest. I keep revisiting my last conversation with Debbie because it's my way of keeping that window open. I don't want to forget my priorities. I want my life to be a more authentic expression of who I am now. I want to challenge the rules and roles that no longer feel right or true. I want to be able to say yes to the wise part of me that keeps asking, *If this were your last day on earth, would you be happy with how you spent it?*

Debbie offered me a sobering dose of reality. In the end there are no marching bands, singing choirs, or mobs of angels celebrating the lives that have been touched by our work. None of that matters. What does matter is love, and truth, and how well we've followed the dictates of the soul.

November 7th

I've been home for a few days now, and I'm settling in. I had a voice lesson today, and when I arrived at Scott's house, he suggested we record the song I've been working on, "Angel from Montgomery." The moment he uttered the word *record*, I froze. Of course he had no way of knowing that his suggestion would set off a storm of emotions inside me. It's been more than three decades since I've stepped foot in a studio, and the last time wasn't pretty. At nineteen, I recorded a song while drinking with friends, and it didn't turn out so well. My boyfriend (the engineer who recorded it) teased me by playing it over and over again the next morning, and I was so embarrassed by how awful I sounded that I vowed never to step into a recording booth again.

Now here I was, almost thirty-five years later, faced with the unexpected opportunity of a do-over.

No sooner was I in Scott's studio than he opened the door to the recording booth and ushered me in. I stepped into the tiny room with its black foam-covered walls and watched silently as Scott set up a music stand, adjusted the microphone, and left the room. I put on my headphones and started to cry. Thank God Scott couldn't see me. While he fiddled with the sound levels in the control room, I made my own adjustments. I placed my hand over my heart and began to talk myself down from the emotional cliff's edge. *You can do this*, I told the little girl inside me who loves to sing. *Just breathe. Let's have fun with this.*

I felt frozen with fear, but it slowly started to melt as I readied myself to begin. Fortunately, I trust Scott. His enthusiasm and playfulness make it easier to face my self-consciousness and fear. And the truth is he really didn't give me time to think about it. Over the next forty-five minutes, we recorded two takes of "Angel from Montgomery," going back to redo any bad notes. Knowing I could fix my mistakes made it easier to enjoy the process; and when we finished, Scott handed me a CD of the recording so I could listen to it in the car.

The CD sat on the passenger seat the whole way back home.

I was too scared to listen. But when I pulled in the driveway, I remembered a promise I'd made to myself after *Take Time for Your Life* was published. Sitting in the parking lot of the post office where I had just picked up a copy sent by a fan who wanted my signature, I glanced through the book and started picking apart my writing. But then something wonderful happened. A firm voice inside me told me to stop, and I knew it represented wisdom. I'd worked too damn hard on that book, I told myself, to go back now and take an inventory of its flaws. In that moment I made a promise to never, ever insult the artist who was brave enough to put her words on paper.

Now I needed to extend the same loving agreement to my singing voice.

I stopped the car at the top of the driveway and popped in the CD. As I sat listening to myself sing, I remembered the story Louise Hay told me about her reaction to giving her very first public talk more than forty years ago. When she stepped offstage and walked to her seat, she silently told herself, *You were fantastic! You were amazing! You couldn't have been better!* She knew that if she criticized her talk,

93

she'd never get on a stage again. So I did my best to listen for everything I loved about my voice. As I got out of the car and walked to the house, I put my hand on my heart. *Thank you,* I said to my brave younger self. *Thank you for trusting me.*

November 8th

I've been feeling frazzled this week, and I haven't felt inspired to write since returning home from New York. I'm edgy and out of sorts, as if my spirit is hovering just outside my body anxiously trying to get back in. It's that existential angst again that has me questioning everything. I continue to wrestle with what matters at this stage of my life. *What secret desires long to see the light of day?* I wonder. *What fantasies and daydreams need to be taken seriously and explored?*

Louise said something to me when we were writing our book that really hit home: "You will be with you longer than anyone else on the planet, so why not make it a good relationship?"

The moment I heard her words, I leaned back in my chair and closed my eyes to take in the full impact of her message. The quality of the relationship we have with ourselves is the foundation upon which we build our entire lives. It determines everything—the choices we make about people, our careers, where we live, and what we will and will not tolerate. As I continue to encourage this good relationship with myself, I'm eager to listen more deeply to the voices that demand to be heard. While I wasn't sure at first why I felt the need to pursue singing, for example, I'm beginning to understand. Taking lessons with Scott has taught me that the creative impulse must be respected and expressed. Not for what it brings us, but for the experience itself and because doing so sends a clear and present message that we are paying attention to the soul.

And I am paying attention.

November 9th

I'm sitting here in my office watching the waning light as the day comes to an end. It's 4:15, and the French doors that lead out to the deck frame the sun as it sinks below the horizon. I stare at the radiant ball of light, willing it to stay in place, but it defies my intent.

Today has been a tender day. I slept very late, then drove to the local healing arts fair to check out the crystals offered by my friend Roberta. On my way there, I played a new song by Christina Aguilera and A Great Big World called "Say

Something." It's gorgeous—simple and raw—and listening to it put me in a state of complete presence, the kind of state Marion Woodman calls "gold dust in the air." With the haunting music echoing in my mind, I walked slowly and deliberately to the church where the fair was being held, taking in my surroundings in a way I rarely do.

So much of feeling alive is about presence, about showing up for life.

Something just caught my attention as I wrote those last words. I looked up to find a young buck frolicking across the field. *Frolicking* doesn't seem like the appropriate word for such a dignified-looking animal, yet it's exactly what he's doing—jumping and running and skipping like a teenager with too much energy on his hands, or should I say hooves. Thank you, God, for this moment of grace—a gift of beauty in a barren landscape hunkering down for winter. I need these moments.

Last night I mustered the courage to invite Bob and Melissa to listen to the song I recorded with Scott in the studio this week. Scott recorded background vocals so the song would sound more professional and sent me the new file in an email. Michael heard it and liked it, so he encouraged me to play it for our friends, and while I was reluctant at first (to say the least), I finally said what the hell and popped in the new CD. They didn't gush (which would have made me horribly uncomfortable), but expressed their genuine surprise and delight at hearing me sing. As they did, I became aware of a little kid inside me jumping up and down, hooting and hollering at having her joy witnessed and affirmed.

I guess I have my own inner frolicking buck, too.

November 10th

Today I made a decision to finally get my office in order. I've been organized and focused for years, handling details with a sense of urgency and commitment. But in the past few months I've been rebelling. It's as if an inner brat has taken over. Emails pile up. I don't care. Phone calls go unreturned. I put them out of my mind. Friends get frustrated because I'm missing in action and I feel bad, but still don't connect. It's as if a part of me finally said, *Enough already. If you can't make time and space to rest and play and explore new creative desires, I'm not going to let you do anything else.*

My inner brat is a formidable presence these days. Like a sentinel at the gate, she stands firm, arms crossed, eyes alert, resolved to stop me from doing anything but tending to my own needs. She's so defiant and strong that I don't have the will to push against her anymore. So I give in. I give in to desire. I give in to sleep. I give in to the daydreaming and the joy of creating something new. It's a mixed bag, this thing called growth. One moment I celebrate the way my life is becoming a more genuine reflection of who I am, and the next I wrestle with the pain of loss as the old me slips away. Death and re-birth. New beginnings and necessary goodbyes.

Early this morning I watched the black silhouette of a lone fisherman casting and recasting his line in the reservoir that sits at the bottom of the hill. As I took in the view, I had a strange sense that my outer world is reflecting my chang-ing inner landscape. The last leaves of autumn are making their inevitable departure, which may be why I've been so fo-cused on death lately. I miss Debbie. I've been missing her all week. Maybe it's the upcoming holiday season. Who knows, it could be the alignment of the stars.

Grief is a funny thing. It sneaks up on you at the most unexpected times. Last night, as I sat in the car waiting for Michael to come out of a drugstore, I turned on the radio just as my new favorite song, "Say Something," began to play. As I sat listening to the words . . .

> *Say something, I'm giving up on you*
> *I'm sorry I couldn't get to you*
> *Anywhere I would've followed you*
> *Say something, I'm giving up on you*

. . . I felt the pain of losing Debbie rush to the surface, and I pressed my lips together in a futile attempt to keep the feelings down. It's heartbreaking to lose someone we love.

Sometimes I feel desperate to know that she's okay, that she's still with me, that there's life beyond the release of the physical body.

I'm waiting for a sign, some irrefutable evidence that her energy and consciousness live on. Silly human that I am . . .

I don't mind the sadness, though. Debbie's death has taught me, once again, that embracing grief and loss strengthens my ability to open my heart to more love. I've grown to trust that I will live through the pain, which frees me to invest more of my heart and soul in the people I care about. And that investment makes me feel more alive, something I want more of in my life.

For some reason grief loves to visit me at the most inconvenient times, though—like this one, when I'm sitting in the car in front of the drugstore waiting for Michael as people walk by. Sometimes I say the hell with it, and just let the tears flow. Usually I don't; I short-circuit my grief in favor of staving off my embarrassment and save the pain for another day. Yet grief doesn't disappear when we push it aside. It lurks in the shadows, waiting for another opportunity to come out and be healed.

Oh well. Today I invite grief in. I welcome its heaviness and pain, its wisdom, its benevolence, and its ability to connect me with my tender heart.

November 11th

My birthday is coming up in a few days, and I've been reflecting on the past year. This birthday is particularly significant since so much has been shifting over the last nine months. Nine months. It seems I'm giving birth to a new version of myself.

I met with my therapist, Sylvia, today, and we talked about how much my life has changed since I started seeing her over a year and a half ago. I live more in the present moment. I have a better sense of what really matters, and I'm honoring it. I'm taking better care of my health by eating well and moving my body. I've accepted that being in nature is a nonnegotiable need, and I want to be home more to experience the beauty of the changing seasons. And most of all, I'm honoring my creative impulses. Crafting and arranging flowerpots on the deck, gardening, writing from a more personal and vulnerable place, singing, and taking a more active role in decorating our home. So many of the things I used to fantasize about doing as I rushed through my hectic, crazy life are now becoming an integral part of my daily routine. It feels good to spend a session reviewing all these positive changes. Stopping along the way to name what's working is just as important as dealing with what needs to be healed.

It's also been a time for saying goodbye. Change on the inside sets in motion change on the outside, and I've had to face the loss of friendship as a result. So much is written about the ending of romantic relationships and very little, if any, about the growing apart of friends. Ever since Suzanne and I parted company, it's been as painful as saying goodbye to a lover. She was a dear, close friend, and after years of sharing our lives, I finally faced the fact that our priorities were no longer in sync. She was spending more and more time focused on building her career when I was more interested in enjoying quality time together.

We did our best to dance around the truth, making plans now and then only to have them fall through, but eventually we had a much-needed come-to-Jesus conversation. Suzanne brought up the tension between us, and I decided to stop pretending. Our friendship seems to have reached a crossroads, I told her, and we need to face the fact that we're heading in different directions. We talked, we cried, and at the end of the call, we decided to formally end the relationship. Although I was tempted to suggest that our friendship might just need to take a new form, I knew better and stopped myself. As difficult as it was to say goodbye, my gut told me it was the right decision. Not only have our priorities changed, but our values have shifted as well. And when values collide, it's hard to move forward together in an honest and meaningful way.

Now I need to continue to grieve, to live with the sadness for as long as it takes. At the same time, I also want to look at what needs to be healed. I want to deal with the old, familiar patterns that were at play again: caretaking in the hopes of feeling loved and valued, trying to become indispensable in order to avoid being abandoned, conversations continually turned toward the other because I'm not comfortable focusing on my own needs. It's hard to admit these things, but they're true. These are the issues I want to work through with Sylvia in therapy, not only so I don't keep repeating these patterns, but also because doing so takes the sting out of my present-day pain.

While life hasn't been easy so far during "the change," it's been authentic, and that's all I can ask for.

November 13th

We just had a new piece of furniture installed in the foyer upstairs, a tall, Gothic mirror shaped like a window. It fits beautifully above the table Michael found online, and I find myself going back to stare at the perfection of it all. It's a destination that invites the soul to stop and have a good drink.

I love the way our home is finally coming together, reflecting the essence of both Michael and me. It's satisfying to see and actually touch something we've envisioned for so long.

This afternoon I feel a bit rushed. After spending yesterday taking my dad to the doctor, I have a lot of catching up to do. I promised Debbie's editor I'd deliver the introduction for the paperback edition of *Courage* by the end of next week. Fortunately I'm feeling pretty good about what I have so far, and I'm glad I've made time to add something to this journal. I don't like to go more than two or three days without writing here.

November 15th

Today is my fifty-fourth birthday, and I woke to a raspberry sherbet sunrise. What a way to start the day. The temperature is going to be in the mid-fifties, so I'll get to spend some time outside, and that makes me happy. I've decided to live spontaneously today. No to-dos to finish, no deadlines to meet. Just doing what I feel moved to do. Poupon is curled up on the old red pillow I placed in the middle of the living room floor so he'd be bathed in a ray of sunlight. Am I the only cat lover who moves the pillow around so he can enjoy the sun as it circles the room?

Later

I did a little shopping earlier and bought myself two dozen peach roses. I'm in love with all shades of orange this year. After filling a vase for my office, I took several roses and placed them individually in the antique glass bottles I've collected over the last few years. I love the variety of colors—sea-foam green, cobalt blue, jeweled amber—and all different sizes. I arranged them on the windowsill behind the kitchen sink like a three-dimensional painting.

After positioning them to my liking, I stood back to admire the beauty. The littlest things can summon such joy.

I'm not sure what I'll do for the rest of the day. Michael is sound asleep upstairs. He has a tooth infection and a fever, and we're waiting to hear from the dentist about an appointment. I have to admit I'm a little disappointed we won't be able to do something special for my birthday. While I'm not a fan of parties, some kind of celebration would be nice.

As I wrote the last line, something remarkable just happened. I suddenly heard a giant *swwwooooossshhhh* and looked up to see a flock of starlings in tight formation not more than twenty feet above my head. Like a school of fish, they moved as one, synchronized flyers putting on a show. As if that wasn't enough, they left a rainbow in their wake.

"Thank you, Mother Nature," I whisper. "I receive your gift with deep gratitude." I'll gladly take that birthday celebration!

November 16th

This morning I set aside time to focus on my annual birthday ritual. I want to go back to last year's journal and find the intentions I set, so I can write about some of what's happened thus far. It's always an eye-opening exercise. Reading words written by my younger self, even if only a year ago, is a humbling experience. I know that last year one of my intentions was to spend more time at home, but when I look back at my schedule, I see that I was in denial about what was coming up on the calendar.

The best intentions do not a healthy life make.

This past year I also wanted to:

> Make our home a more beautiful, peaceful place to live
>
> Experience greater closeness with Michael
>
> Take better care of my body

I'm happy to see that these intentions are fully under way.

Our home is coming along nicely. My office is now finally finished and looks like the warm and inviting salon I envisioned. Every time I walk into the room, I smile at the elegance of it all. The walls are pale salmon in color, and the tall window that overlooks the reservoir is framed in peach fabric, gathered at the top by the gold crown my friend Jacalyn gave us as a housewarming gift. I've done away with my desk, filing cabinet, and work tables, replacing them with a cream-colored love seat, two comfy velvet chairs, and an antique, burled-wood French armoire that keeps my work supplies out of sight. Rarely a day goes by when I don't thank God for this serene and healing space.

My office reflects three things I value deeply: simplicity, order, and beauty. Simplicity helps to create order, and having everything in its place makes me feel peaceful and at ease. And then there's beauty. I'm beginning to realize that beauty is a fundamental value, the essential ingredient of a deeply satisfying life. Whether I'm giddy at the sight of a vibrant red cardinal at the feeder, taken by the stylish lines of a classic dress, or moved by a romantic painting of a stormy sea, beauty is sunlight for my soul.

My relationship with Michael has improved in important ways this year, too. Marriage is hard work. Sharing a life with someone who is also committed to crafting a truly intimate relationship isn't easy. Everything that happens between us becomes fodder for growth, but only through conscious effort. As we've faced our challenges head-on with presence and an ongoing commitment to flourish as a couple, we've grown closer and each of us has become whole as individuals.

The level of intimacy in our marriage was a big issue this past year—for the last few years, actually. Michael and I have had different needs concerning sex, in what seems like a common struggle between men and women. As my workload increased, he felt lonely and hungry for a stronger connection, but I was exhausted and too cut off from myself to reach out to him.

I became the woman I often see in my workshops who's so overwhelmed by daily life that her interest in sex takes a vacation. I tried to pass this off as perimenopause, but deep down I knew the truth. Michael's clear requests for connection, affection, and sex challenged me to face a whole host of issues I'd been working hard to avoid.

I needed to be honest with myself first and foremost. Was I harboring some unconscious anger or resentment, and withholding sex to punish? Maybe. Was I no longer attracted to him physically? No. One look still cast the same spell it did the day we first met. The problem was far more complicated. My schedule was booked in advance, and I couldn't see a way to plan for immediate downtime. I'd put on 20 pounds from eating on the road and exercising sporadically, and it certainly didn't make me feel good about myself, let alone sexy. I was struggling on the inside, too. My emotions were all over the place, overwhelmed one minute, resentful the next, excited about my work, then guilty for not being home. I knew I needed to slow down and get help, but I wasn't good at asking for it, especially in a crisis.

The tension grew so thick between us that it became clear that I needed to take action or I'd risk losing my marriage. I was becoming another statistic—a woman with a husband who routinely complained about not having enough sex—and

I didn't like it. And this is where I come to the point that's important to me. We marginalize women by feeding this myth. It's much easier to play the role of the busy woman who sees sex as one more item on an already unmanageable to-do list, as many women tell me they do, than it is to look more closely at what's really going on.

Of course there are hormonal issues that lower, or eliminate, libido. I'd experienced this imbalance myself and knew it was part of the problem. And yes, most women will admit that they're exhausted. Studies show that women still shoulder the major responsibility for running the household and caring for children, in spite of working more than full time. We keep taking charge and then become encased in an armor of resentment without a clue as to how to take it off.

I was that woman, constantly complaining about how much I handled, rarely asking for support. As far as I was concerned, there were plenty of legitimate reasons for this: I was too busy to find the right help; I was convinced that no one could effectively handle the things that were important to me; I was afraid of being let down if I did try to delegate. And there was something else going on: I was completely disconnected from pleasure. I fantasized about doing things I missed, like going for long hikes, traveling for fun instead of work, entertaining friends in our home, or visiting museums and attending theater performances with Michael—things we used to love to do—but pleasure felt like a luxury. I couldn't afford the time.

So in an attempt to face the issue, I tried something completely out of character. Inspired by a story I read online about a woman who had sex with her husband every day for a year, I decided to try a modified version. I would say yes to Michael's invitations, whether I felt in the mood or not, and see what happened. I never said a word to him about my decision, and he didn't ask. We just enjoyed our time together.

At first it was tough. I'd learned to associate anxiety and stress with having sex because it had become a point of contention between us. I had to embrace these uncomfortable feelings and show up anyway. Fortunately, it didn't take long to get over my discomfort. No sooner were we rolling in the hay than I'd remember how much I loved sex with Michael and wonder why we didn't do it more often.

Slowly I discovered that the more I said yes, the more I wanted to say yes, and the desire for sensual pleasure has only increased. Rather than jump out of bed to get an early start in the office, I'm learning to stay put and enjoy our physical connection. Instead of rushing to empty my inbox before the end of the workday, I'm taking breaks and inviting Michael to join me for an afternoon tryst. And as I've tried this new approach, something unexpected has happened. My body is waking up. Not only am I interested in sex again, I feel more connected to my own sensuality. Physical pleasure is awakening in me the desire for more pleasure in general.

In the meantime, our improved sex life has added a new level of sweetness to our relationship. As silly as it sounds, I hadn't realized how important regular sex is to the emotional intimacy of a marriage. I feel closer to Michael, and he feels closer to me. I think about him more often during the day, smiling to myself at the memory of our lovemaking. I feel inspired to do little unexpected things for him, just to let him know how much he means to me. And I receive the same from him—a text telling me he loves me or a spontaneous reach for my hand, the kind of reach that says, *You're mine, and I'm happy about that.* Spending more time together in bed has made us both feel more loved, desired, and appreciated—and it's spilling over into other areas of our lives.

My health has also improved. I've lost fifteen pounds, have been drinking more green juice than I ever thought possible, and have worked out nearly every day for the last eight months. My sister Kerri has been a godsend—a walking partner and trusted companion on this path of healing. It's made a world of difference to have her support.

I'm letting go of the need to push my way through life. Instead, I'm learning to relax and be more receptive to what life brings to me. Yes, I'm becoming the chalice instead of the gladiator, the prize itself instead of the warrior who fights for it.

As I look ahead to the coming year, these are my new intentions:

To continue on the healing path to live peacefully in my body

To finish this journal and decide if it's meant to be published

To explore new professional interests

To finish decorating our home

To continue to deepen my relationship with Michael

Happy Birthday, Cheryl. I'm glad you're here!

November 21st

This morning I felt another little shift. My body is relaxing into winter, rather than hoping for one last warm autumn day.

I finally finished the draft of Debbie's new intro, and I hope her editor likes it. Writing this has been an emotional struggle. I was asked to share something personal, yet her death is still fresh, and I feel protective of both Debbie and our relationship. I could never betray our conversations or the intimate process she went through when leaving her physical body. And neither Debbie's life nor her work lend themselves to superficial comments. She was extraordinary in her capacity to dig deep into the psyche and pull up pain that needed to be released. Her work needs to be experienced to be fully understood, and words can't come close to doing it justice. Still I hope I've managed to contribute in some small way to the ongoing success of her book.

Now I'm free to work on other projects and continue with this journal. Winter is a good time to write, a time when the energy of the world is a bit dimmer and less intrusive.

November 25th

It is another stunning day, and the reservoir is brimming with light. I woke this morning in good spirits, until I read a blog post written by a colleague, a woman I respect who writes and speaks about similar topics. She's hip and smart, and she has a wonderful, unique voice. I felt hit by a wave of jealousy as I read her words, a creeping insecurity rising up within me. No sooner did I finish the piece than my inner critic started in: *Your time has come and gone. Move over. This woman is the new kid in town. You're old news.*

Ugh.

I *am* getting older, and the role of elder is a new one for me. Historically I've always been the youngest of my peers and colleagues, especially in the early stages of my career. In my twenties I worked in finance, then a male-dominated field where I was surrounded by older men. Years later, when I moved into consulting and coaching, I still found myself on the younger side of the crowd. I remember a boss from one of my corporate gigs asking me to keep the few early gray hairs I had so I'd appear older than my years when counseling executives. Now I *am* older, and it makes me edgy and uncomfortable. If I'm going to stay committed to living consciously, however, I'll need to deal with these feelings head-on.

It doesn't help that my priorities are changing. While I don't want to be perceived as outdated and irrelevant, the truth is I'm more into presence these days and less into performance. My career as a writer and speaker has far exceeded my expectations, and I'm grateful for that. But the voice of the gladiator tells me I'm supposed to want more—to book the next TV show or speaking engagement, or climb the bestseller lists. But I'm not the same woman. The thought of going back to the pace I used to keep feels intolerable. Today my ego is taking a backseat to my soul, and my soul tells me there's a different way to move forward. I have to be brave, to slow down, to create space, and to look honestly at what I want at this point in my life. Then I'll know how I want the next stage of my career to unfold.

Yes, this is a new season.

While there are times when I notice wrinkles and a growing interest in comfortable clothes, I have to admit that physical aging has been the least of my concerns—at least so far, anyway. My commitment to my inner life has created a healthy distraction from that worry. A discomfort with aging shows up more when it comes to my work. The marketplace is always looking for shiny and new, and that's just not me anymore. And while I know my insatiable curiosity and passion for growth will certainly keep me relevant, I'm more concerned with staying true to the work than with fame or monetary success. I long for the old days when the writing and teaching of people like Marion Woodman, Robert Bly, and Robert A. Johnson took center stage. They were wisdom teachers who were passionate about poetry, literature, depth psychology, and the path of the soul. They taught from a well of insight that was both personal and universal. To them, the shiny object was the spiritual journey itself.

As I read over this entry I find both truth and traces of defensiveness. Aging with integrity is a challenge. I think I'm up to it, but sometimes I have to admit that this consciousness work sucks.

November 26th

Ileen arrived last night from London, and the house is full of life and laughter. It's fitting that she would come for the week of Thanksgiving, since that's the traditional time when our soul family gets together. I'll be cooking a big feast on Thursday for me, Michael, Ileen, Robin and Larry, and Max. I also invited Scott when I heard his family plans fell through at the last minute. I have no doubt he'll fit right in.

I'm sitting by the window in my office feeling tired. It's a cold, beige day, the listless fields and empty trees dark against the blank sky. A flock of starlings just flew over the reservoir—a purposeful act in an otherwise dormant, brooding landscape.

November 27th

It's 4:30 a.m., and two events have conspired to interrupt my sleep. One is my damn nocturnal roommate, Poupon, meowing with a toy in his mouth. The other is the noisy thrumming of a hard rain. Under other circumstances I might find it soothing, but I can't stop thinking about the leak in my office. It's been here since before we finished building, and we still can't find the source. We had a pesky leak in the last house, too, so I close my eyes and tune in to my intuition to see why this keeps happening. The answer comes immediately: *You always need something to worry about.*

It's true. I'm temperamentally anxious. There are deep neural pathways carved out long ago that run an old program designed to search for the worst-case scenario, and it's times like this when I must intervene on my own behalf. I need to turn this problem over to Larry, our handyman, and let him handle it. I'm going to resist the temptation to toss and turn for the rest of the night over the thought of water soaking into our walls. This time I'm choosing peace.

November 28th

I woke up early after a solid night's sleep to run a trail race with my sister Kerri and her wife, Missy. There were well over a thousand people in attendance at Maudslay State Park's 5K Turkey Trot. Before I left the house, Michael said two things that saved me during the race: "First, start out slow and pace yourself. Second, remember your mantra."

Healthy, strong body is the phrase I learned from a woman who does energy work on cats. Last year I watched a video where she rubs the body of the cat in a circular motion while repeating this mantra and it helps to strengthen their health and constitution. After seeing the effectiveness of her work, I began using the mantra myself when I got tired walking or jogging up hills.

Running this race was a big deal for me because it's a sign that my daily exercise routine over the last year has paid off. I ran the whole thing, up and down hills and through the woods. Toward the end, when I thought I was going to poop out, I started using the mantra over and over again. *Healthy, strong body. Healthy, strong body. Healthy, strong body.* Jogging up the hill toward the finish line (who puts a finish line on a hill?!), I smiled to myself as I passed the big digital clock tracking the time. I'm in better shape now than I have been in years.

Later

Thanksgiving dinner was a success! We had an organic turkey for the carnivores and plenty of yummy vegetables for the vegetarians. We laughed and told stories and enjoyed all the delicious food, and now tomorrow's feast is set. In keeping with Mom's tradition, I'll take all of the leftovers—turkey, sweet potatoes, Brussels sprouts, spinach, butternut squash, and gravy—and mix them all together in a large frying pan. Ileen, Michael, and I will enjoy it for lunch tomorrow (and maybe even dinner, too!).

December 2nd

Life is changing. *I'm* changing. As I face the reality that life as I've known it no longer works for me, I'm confronting a stream of feelings about getting older, leaving dreams behind, saying goodbye to people and plans and goals. In some ways I'm emptying my life to claim space for something I can't yet name, guided only by the desire to express myself in new and different ways.

Ever since I was twelve years old, I've called myself a writer. The title felt legit. I didn't need to publish a book or have a byline in a magazine. As far as I was concerned, the fact that I kept a journal and wrote in it nearly every day gave me license to call myself a writer. Calling myself an artist, however, has been a different story. Michael is an artist. He started cartooning in grade school and continues to this day. He also has a gift for architecture and design that is reflected in every room of our home. He's always been the artist in the family.

Until now.

Years ago during a family reunion, my brother-in-law Walter did something that roused a sleeping part of me. He created a fun family game, a treasure hunt of sorts, with personalized name tags, and when he handed me mine, it read, "Artist." I looked at Walter, looked at the name tag, then looked back at him to be sure he'd given it to the right person. When he nodded, I stuck it to the front of my shirt. As soon as I did, something weird happened. I had a vision of a little girl jumping up and down yelling, "Yes! Yes! Yes!" That name tag was an invitation, a call to reclaim a part of me that was clearly eager for attention.

It was an invitation I ignored for the next fifteen years.

Fast-forward to the present moment. When Chris Northrup said that issues that hadn't been resolved during adolescence would come around again during perimenopause, she wasn't kidding. I'm confronted with the lifelong patterns that need to be healed and released—like trying to rescue people who don't want to be rescued, or giving in the hopes of feeling worthy of love. Confronting these patterns has also forced me to confront the parts of me that are arrogant (I know what others need), manipulative (I try to get them to see it), and codependent (I care more about keeping others happy at the expense of my own contentment).

As unattractive as these parts are, I've held on to them. Who would I be without the roles that have defined me for most of my life?

Chris also said that when a woman deals with these unresolved issues, she has a good chance of reconnecting with the dreams that ignited her heart during the tumultuous passage of puberty. From what I can tell, these are the joyful, engaged parts of us that often get submerged by parents who push us to travel a responsible road, or by an educational system designed to produce compliance and conformity.

I'm getting reacquainted with that young girl. Turns out she is an artist, one who likes to paint with words.

Yes, I'm a writer. The blank page is my canvas. Words are my paint, my pastels, my pens. But I'm also a woman who loves to express her creativity in a variety of ways. Singing for the sheer joy of it. Transforming my office into a sensual salon. Indulging my love of fashion by choosing clothes that reflect who I am today, not who I thought I should be. A sensual woman living a sensual life.

We all want to experience the magic of losing ourselves to something larger than we are, something mysterious and light filled and transcendent. That's what being an artist is all about. My artist is my lifeline to truth. She's my lifeline to joy and meaning. She's my lifeline to my *self*.

Later

I took the journal entry I wrote today and used it to craft a blog post for my online community. Tonight I received an email from my dad telling me how impressed he was by it. My eyes filled with tears as I read his words. Years of therapy and honest, hard-to-have conversations have left us with a relationship I value deeply. I appreciated his email and am still surprised that Mom and Dad read my blogs, let alone comment on them. I don't care how old I am, there's still a kid inside who longs to be seen by her parents.

And I am.

December 5th

It's a foggy day in the most romantic way. Smoky clouds drifting just above the trees are reflected in the still, calm water of the reservoir. The whole scene is bathed in a silver light that changes moment to moment as the clouds shift and move. I could stare at this painting for hours . . .

We're into the holiday season, and I have to be careful about overwhelming myself by allowing a ticker tape of to-dos to scroll through my head. There are presents to buy, cards to send, packages to ship. But this year I'm calming my anxieties by doing something different. I've decided to share the wealth (as Michael would say) by hiring a part-time assistant to help with projects and errands, and after the first day of receiving her support, I already feel relieved. I also feel challenged. Today I caught myself driving to the store for cat food after I included it on the list for my new assistant. I actually pulled into the parking lot, telling myself it would only take a few minutes, but then I made myself pull right back out. These "it will just take a few minutes" activities add up to hours of time I'd rather spend in other ways, and having someone else do them provides extra income for people who really apreciate it.

December 8th

Last night we hosted a holiday party for my family, and it was the first time in years that my siblings and parents gathered as a group without grandchildren or other guests. It was just us, and it was a big success. Michael decorated the house in his simple and elegant way, dimming the lights, placing tea candles on tables and mantels, and illuminating the angel statues around the house with warm candlelight from the tall church candelabras set up on the floor. Two friends who have a small catering business, Jim and Marilyn, came to cook the meal, and they really helped make the evening special.

We laughed, sang songs, drank wine, and enjoyed a delicious feast of prime rib, roasted potatoes, green beans amandine, and Christmas cake. After dinner I arranged for the meaningful gift swap Michael and I have made a tradition over the years, and I was pleased to see that everyone took it seriously. I had asked people to bring one small gift with some kind of special significance for them. After dinner we retired to the living room, and I numbered the presents and set them on the floor in a long line. I put a second set of numbers in a hat, and as we went around the room each person pulled a number and chose the corresponding gift. Then we all watched as, one by one, each person opened their gift and listened as the giver shared the meaning behind it.

It's always wonderful to hear the stories of why people give what they do. I was touched by my brother-in-law Mark, who talked about feeling disappointed that his father, a big baseball fan, died before he could experience the joy of watching the Red Sox win the World Series in 2004. Mark's gift was a Red Sox Christmas ornament. My dad's decision to give away one of his Korean War medals took all of us by surprise. His voice was thick with emotion as he talked about what it was like to live on a troopship crossing the Pacific at seventeen years old. My sister Donna was the grateful recipient of his medal. She then offered Michael her gift—a yoga mat, representing the place where she says she feels most centered and at peace. My sister-in-law Janice, who has a passion for interior design, chose my gift of a small statue dedicated to the healing power of beauty, and I received a gratitude journal from my sister Michelle. I'll be sure to fill it with plenty of worthy examples over the next year.

How long have I dreamt about having room in my calendar, in my life, to do something like this? To plan a party, design a meal, decorate the house, and host a truly meaningful family experience?

Michael and I spent an hour cleaning up after everyone left, comparing observations on the party and sharing stories. I felt so supported by him throughout the evening. At one point I looked over and felt my heart well up with such love for this man who is my family. We're settling into our relationship in a new way now that we don't have to hold our breath worrying about me leaving anytime soon. After twenty years, I'm grateful to still feel like the luckiest woman in the world.

Later

Michael is at the New England Patriots game, and I'm home alone enjoying the afternoon to myself. Even though our sleep schedules support our independent natures, I still covet my time alone here. As a young girl, I found solace in solitude. My sanctuary, a small bedroom of my own, was a treasured gift I finally received when I turned thirteen and Dad bought the old colonial house in Medway. It was the one place I could get away from the noise and chaos of a large family.

Much like the need for beauty, I'm also growing to appreciate my need for space. I plan to take a hot bath, read a good book, and see where my imagination wants to take me.

December 9th

This morning I woke to a slow, gentle snow dressing the tree branches just outside my window in a lacy, white coat. As I stare out at the tall pine trees and sturdy oaks, I appreciate the beauty, but I can also feel the tug of winter dragging me down. I know how cold it must be outside and my body doesn't want to move, yet my mind longs for the stimulation of the world. It's that old, familiar tension again between the part of me who wants to move beyond these walls and the part who wants to hole up and hide.

Hibernation has been winning more often than not these days. Michael and I decided to cancel the trip to New York we planned for the day after Christmas. I don't want to pack another damn suitcase, and I do want the emotional and physical space to write. Writing is my meditation, my spiritual practice. I need space to work without interruption, time to mine for gold in the stillness.

December 11th

It has been bleak and wintry for the past five days. And dark. Yesterday I took the light box out and set it on the table in my office so I'd be bathed in brightness while I worked. Within twenty minutes I felt better. Today, however, I won't need the box. The clouds have vanished, and the snowy landscape shimmers in the sunlight. As soon as I finish here, I intend to go for a long walk. Fall was so mild that I got used to heading out in a T-shirt and yoga pants. Now I need to learn a new way of dealing with the cold so I can continue to move my body. I'm feeling good, and I want to keep it up.

My success with exercising consistently stemmed from my decision to look for enjoyable ways to move my body. Early on I tried to convince myself that if I could only adhere to a strict fitness program, I'd lose weight and silence the brutal voice in my head that relentlessly judged my body. I thank Geneen Roth, both for her book *Women Food and God*, and for reminding me that any weight-loss program based on deprivation rather than inquiry and understanding was doomed to fail. Reaching my ideal weight seven years ago only to gain it all back and then some was devastating. This time I'm looking for a loving and compassionate relationship with my body, one rooted in a commitment to be present to my feelings. By paying attention to what's going on for me emotionally each time I want to eat (when I'm not really hungry), I've developed a new kind of relationship with food. When my mind tells me I'm hungry but my body doesn't agree, I ask myself: *What am I feeling right now? What am I trying to avoid? What's missing that I think food can replace?* This new approach is built on kindness, curiosity, and tenderness toward myself, and that's a program I can sustain.

December 12th

I woke this morning to a herd of deer in the backyard, the first time I've seen more than one or two in a long time. I ran through the house like a wild woman looking for my camera (feeling grateful to Scott for its telephoto lens). I was able to take several shots before they jumped over the stone wall and disappeared from view. One photo is of a young buck. His antlers are short, maybe six inches or so, and he stares directly into the camera, warm breath misting in the frosty air. Wow, he is stunning.

As I type these words my fingers are starting to throb. With the cold, wet weather settling in, the arthritis in my hands has been acting up. I need to take photos so I can email them to our friend Jay, who's a hand surgeon, and find out what's going on. I've been reluctant to do this for two reasons. First, I know how my mind works when it comes to health issues. A scary diagnosis or a possible worst-case scenario tends to get stuck in my head and then plays like a scratched record, over and over again.

Second, I don't want to face the fact that I might have any physical limitations as I get older. I want to believe that I can be fit and strong and unencumbered till the day I die. I also have this twisted thought that I can make the problem go away by refusing to address it, but that's not working. Denial is a silly form of therapy.

Visualizing healthy, pain-free hands will certainly help, but I also need to find out what's going on. I'm allowing myself to gently come to terms with the need to do something about this.

December 15th

A big snowstorm came through last night, and it's a day to stay in my pajamas, enjoy tea, and putter around doing the little things that I love to do without any agenda or plan. Reminds me of being a kid in a way, although downtime wasn't really celebrated in our busy household.

Yesterday morning I woke at 7 a.m. with a start. Michael let me know that his mom, Pat, had fallen and broken her shoulder. I sat bolt upright as he explained that she'd been in the hospital all night without our knowing about it. Michael was upset. His brother said they sent a text, but I'm not sure what happened because we never received it.

I jumped up and began getting dressed. Michael was a little surprised by my reaction, and, truth be told, I was, too. That's the funny thing about an accident, sudden illness, or death—it gives us an instant perspective on how important someone is to us. And Pat is important to me. We got to the hospital before 8 a.m. and stayed to meet with the doctor at noon. It turned out that she'd broken her shoulder in several places and dislocated the humerus bone. Fortunately, there's a good chance she won't need surgery, just a brief period under anesthesia to relocate the bone, which will happen on Wednesday.

Both Michael and I have always seen our mothers as solid fixtures in our lives, and this experience was a stark reminder of their vulnerability. And ours. We've been blessed with very few deaths in our lives, but we know that's going to change. Thank God we have each other.

December 16th

The days are getting darker, winter is taking over, and I can feel my vitality ebbing. I hate it. My energy is my greatest asset, and it has always been a challenge to surrender to a dip. The winter solstice is approaching, as well as a full moon. At least the solstice ushers in the shortest day of the year, and that means more light is on the way.

Poupon is howling from the living room. He's having a grand old time running from window to window, chasing the melting snow as it slides off the metal rooftop and lands on the deck below. Lurking along the back of the sofa, he watches the roofline like a hawk, waiting for a clump of snow to drop. When it does he lunges at the window trying to grab it. The first time I saw him do it, I rushed to stop him because I thought he might get hurt, but not our boy. He's strong and resilient, not to mention persistent. And he seems so happy I can't bring myself to interfere.

Like an unconscious habit, Poupon is woven into the fabric of our lives. I wake in the morning and usually find him somewhere near, curled up under my arm or lying in the crook of my knee. As I move through the house, my legs naturally accommodate his small body, reflexively moving this way and that to avoid running him over. His feeding times are scheduled on a synchronized internal clock that draws us both into the kitchen at the same time, and we communicate with growing proficiency. When I'm ready for sleep and he's not around, I telepathically invite him to join me. Within a few minutes I hear the little "urt" sound he makes as he jumps up on the nightstand—his way of letting me know he's received the signal.

I've been sleeping alone, and I appreciate Poupon's company now and then. I made the decision to move into the guest bedroom to escape the white noise machine and blowing fans that Michael needs to sleep. As a result, I've been able to get more rest, and I feel so much better. It was an important act of self-care to choose to set up my own room, but not an easy decision. Michael wasn't happy, and the truth is I wasn't either. I love sleeping next to him. I feel closer and more connected when we're able to be together. But I also love to sleep, and as we've gotten older, our needs have changed. He prefers a cave-like atmosphere that's dark and noisy and windy. I need silence, fresh air, and uncovered windows that stay open to catch the morning light.

I've also needed a room of my own, just like I did when I was thirteen. I think every woman does—a place to escape to, to retreat from the physical and energetic pull of others, a private haven to rest and think and dream. It's not a very popular choice, however. As soon as Michael and I made the decision to create our own "chambers," I began to hear about what a grave decision it is for couples to not sleep together. No doubt an outer reflection of my inner concern. One morning, I turned on the TV to find a well-known male talk-show host advising a couple against separate bedrooms. "It will damage your marriage," he asserted. I smiled and changed channels, thinking how outdated his reaction was . . . and how patriarchal. As a woman creates and inhabits her own space, she draws more power into her being. Pretty scary stuff for the old boys. Besides, both Michael and I have, once again, found a way to make this new arrangement work.

What good is a marriage if the individuals who make up the partnership are not allowed to do what they need to do to move toward wholeness? Enjoying a space of my own supports me in important ways. I can think for myself. I can digest and process my day. I can pray, write, cry, toss and turn, and do what I need to do to make sense of this crazy existence. My bedroom is a sanctuary, a sacred place that returns me to myself. Michael would say I'm much better to be with because of it, too. It's just another way we're using our partnership for support as we continue to amend our traditional tribal rules.

December 17th

Okay, it's a little too early in winter for minus four degrees outside! My body and mind are revolting. As much as I love New England, this could be a deal breaker. I've begun fantasizing about soft sand beaches in Mexico, visiting friends in San Diego, and surfing Airbnb's website for seaside bungalows on the southern coastline.

The pain in my hands and arms has increased, too, and I'm scared. It seems to have gotten worse in the past few days, and I've already jumped ahead to the possibility of losing my ability to use them for good. Last night I had Michael take pictures of my hands while at the restaurant waiting for dinner to be served. I need to finally send them to Jay. When I glanced at the photos, tears sprung to my eyes and Michael took note. He reached across the table, folded my hands into his, looked directly into my eyes, and said, "Don't worry, honey, we'll get to the bottom of this and find out exactly what we need to do to fix it."

I believe him. He's my knight in shining armor.

December 19th

Michael's mother came through her surgical procedure with flying colors. The doctor was able to reposition the bone without an incision, and she's home resting. Well, maybe not resting. That's not in her nature. She's like me. She needs to be moving, and she's frustrated with not being able to do much. Pat values her independence and dreads the prospect of losing it.

Last night, while Michael caught up on sleep after spending the day at the hospital, I did something I've wanted to do for a while now. I unpacked a special box that's been sitting in the guest-room closet for a long time. The box was filled with objects from the old meditation space in our house on Ferry Road. There were so many items I'd forgotten about, and the most surprising was a long, elegant hand holding a candle that Debbie had given me years ago. As I unwrapped the paper and discovered it, tears sprang to my eyes, and I remembered her instructions: *work less, take more vacations, embrace greedy.*

God, I miss her.

Once I emptied the box, I created a new space to pray and meditate. I hung a favorite picture of Mother Mary on the wall and then placed several items on a table in front of her: a statue of Jesus, a smiling Buddha, my highlighted copy of the

Bhagavad Gita, a sweet picture of Paramahansa Yogananda along with his powerful book *Autobiography of a Yogi*, the one that introduced me to Hinduism and the practice of meditation. Seeing it reminds me to read it again. Each time I do, I feel changed on a cellular level by the consciousness in his writing.

I also put out the wedding photo of Michael and me, along with a copy of the vows he wrote for our ceremony. Finally, over the picture of Mary, I hung a set of antique rosary beads from Lucy (a deceased friend), and the Virgin Mary scapular I found next to my car the day I asked the Divine Mother for support while facing a difficult situation with a neighbor.

It's good to have a new spiritual home.

December 22nd

I woke up this morning with an agenda that was interrupted by Michael. I had planned to work on my blog post, wrap some Christmas presents, and go for a walk, but he invited me to crawl back into bed with him instead. In the past I would have declined as graciously as I could in order to stay on task, but things are different now. My decision to say yes to his intimate invitations is a statement to him and myself that I'm making my marriage more of a priority. And that choice has been wonderful for our relationship. So I crawled back into bed.

Michael's willingness to take a stand about sex has forced me to grow in surprising ways. What began as a problem turned out to be a doorway leading to a deeper understanding of myself as a woman. I'm beginning to see sex as a form of expression that's vital to our marriage *and* to me, as well as symbolic of my larger relationship with pleasure in general. After all, if I say no to Michael's invitation, I have to look at what I'm saying yes to. Housework, getting things done in the office, or another trip to teach is becoming a secondary priority, taking a backseat to connection and intimacy. As a result, not only do I feel more interested in sex, I'm finding more joy in other sensual pleasures—sunbathing on the deck, long walks in the middle of the day, a hot bath before dinner, or hosting a delicious impromptu meal on the veranda with friends.

So this morning, as I lay in bed with Michael after a beautiful session of lovemaking, I feel more strongly than ever that we do ourselves (and our partners) a disservice by perpetuating this myth that women are less interested in sex than men. I find that message offensive and disempowering. Both men and women long for connection, a feeling of partnership, and a deep sense of belonging to each other. What we women really need is to reawaken to the importance of pleasure. At least that's what I need. It's not only bringing me (us) great sex; it's bringing me a great life.

December 25th

It's Christmas day, and this morning I woke up to watch the sunrise. I slept next to Michael last night, and he was gently snoring beside me with Poupon nestled in between his legs in a pool of soft, new light. I wrapped myself in my old blue sweater, grabbed my laptop, and came downstairs to make a cup of tea and write in the living room.

Yesterday, in an attempt to do Christmas differently this year, Michael and I spent the afternoon at Wentworth by the Sea, a cozy island hotel in the town of New Castle, overlooking the Atlantic Ocean. After lunch at their new restaurant, Salt, we toasted each other with champagne during pedicures, which were followed by massages. Such fun!

By the time we left the Wentworth it was dark, and against the inky backdrop of the night sky, the Christmas decorations outside the massive hotel were magnificent. I loved the giant sleigh filled with gifts and twinkling multicolored lights parked at the entrance. Driving over the little bridge that connects New Castle to the larger world, we discovered luminescent bags lit by candles lining both sides of the street. The tiny pools of light flowed alongside us for a mile or so, and all the while we oohed and aahed like delighted children. "This is one of those experiences we'll remember for the rest of our lives," I said to Michael as the candlelight faded in the distance. "Yes," he replied, "these moments are what life's all about."

Our dear friend Max showed up at seven for dinner, and the three of us ate next to a roaring fire. Later, after Max went home, Michael and I fell into bed, grateful for our day and what might become a new family tradition.

December 28th

It's been a busy couple of days getting ready for Ileen's arrival and helping out Michael's mother. Her shoulder is coming along nicely, and I've been replacing bandages and washing her hair. I'm getting pretty good at styling it. The first time I tried was an awkward experience, juggling the brush and the hair dryer. The next time, as I relaxed, I found myself moving my hands and the equipment in a more natural way, and it became fun. Pat was happy with the results, too.

It's such an intimate experience to wash someone's hair or replace bandages on their wound. I know Pat's not used to letting someone get so close, and I did my best to be sensitive to this new arrangement. I spoke to her in a gentle tone, asking for feedback, and offering reassurance along the way. She's a proud, confident woman who's used to being in charge, and I certainly know what that's like. I have to say, though, she was surprisingly quick to let the awkwardness melt into receptivity. It was a lesson for me in receiving graciously, and this experience has certainly brought us closer together.

December 30th

I'm sitting in bed next to Michael as he sleeps. Last night I crawled in next to him to talk about our day and wound up dozing off and staying put. It's so nice to sleep together now and then. A few minutes ago he woke up, looked over at me working on the laptop, then took in the rosy orange light glowing on the horizon. Without missing a beat he said, "It's a watercolor parfait." Then he made a goofy face, rolled over, and fell back asleep. He loves to tease me. Actually, I think he lives to tease me.

We're getting close to the end of the year, and I couldn't be happier. This past year hasn't been easy. As the structures that have supported my life thus far are beginning to fall away, I'm left feeling both shaky and excited. Life, I imagine, is making way for something new. Friendships have ended, my relationship with Michael is growing and evolving, work is changing, and my calendar feels more spacious. It hasn't been comfortable learning to sit in this new space, but I'm gradually getting used to it. I like the life that's rising from the ashes of the old.

Thus far the benefits are:

More time at home

A deeper connection with Michael

More time with family and friends (and Poupon)

A delicious feeling of satisfaction from my new creative endeavors, musical and literary

A healthier body

Lots of time outdoors

A life less roiled by drama

A young man who has called in to my radio show several times in the past posted a comment on Facebook. Turns out he's a Chinese astrologer, and he read a blog post I wrote about all the changes going on in my life. "Last year was the year of the snake," he wrote, "and it's your opposing sign." He went on to tell me that we're headed into the year of the horse, a much better sign for him, and for me, too.

I'll take that good news!

December 31st

Today is the last day of the year, and for me this is always a time for introspection. I've spent the morning reviewing the last twelve months with all its changes and challenges, heartaches and growth. Tonight we're having a dinner party, an intimate gathering with a few close friends, and I'm feeling both melancholy and hopeful. The wistfulness comes from the goodbyes I've had to say this past year. I'll miss Suzanne. She often spent the holidays with us, and this year will feel strange without her.

When an important relationship ends, I often question myself. It's hard to walk the same path with someone for years, come to a crossroads, and make a choice to go in a different direction. At times I still wonder: *Was I too quick to turn the page? Couldn't I have just accepted a new version of the friendship and continued on? If not, why did I call this person into my life in the first place, and have I learned the lessons he or she presented?*

Friendship, like any relationship, is a gift *and* a catalyst for important work—inner development that, ultimately, may have nothing to do with the actual person. Perspective can be healing. As I look back over the pain and suffering that accompanied the end of our friendship, I see Suzanne as a spiritual actor in the divine play of this lifetime. Hurt is turning into gratitude for the healing that's taken place. I like to imagine that she feels this way, too.

Some endings are necessary in order to move on to the next stage of one's life.

So if sadness springs from what's lost, hope comes from knowing that this past year has set the stage for deeper satisfaction with my life. This is the first New Year in a long time when I haven't felt unhappy being in my body, when I'm making no resolution to lose weight. Instead, I'm gradually returning to a natural, healthy size by being more physically active and by learning to use food for physical nourishment instead of using it to manage uncomfortable feelings. I exercised earlier today, and I've done so nearly every day for the last eight months. It's been one of the most important gifts I've given myself this year—physical movement as a daily, spiritual practice. The new confidence and the kindness I feel toward myself has been well worth the effort, discipline, and commitment.

Tonight I'm looking forward to a quiet time with friends.

January 1st

Last night I didn't get to bed until 2:30 a.m., something I rarely do these days. The evening was great fun, though. Ileen brought an advance copy of *The Wolf of Wall Street*, and we

141

watched it while waiting for Max to arrive. With its brilliant script and excellent acting, the film is a nonstop assault on the viewer's senses and sensibilities. We were exhausted by the final frame.

When I think about this coming year I don't feel inspired to set goals or intentions. Instead, I want to place my attention on how I'd like to *feel*.

> I want to feel comfortable in my body—healthy, fit, and strong.
>
> I want to feel excited and stimulated by the company I keep.
>
> I want to feel moved and inspired by my writing and teaching.
>
> I want to feel spiritually connected to nature.
>
> I want to feel a deep love for Michael, and for our friends.
>
> I want to feel fed by my creative process.
>
> I want to feel free and spacious in my life.

As I look back over this list, I think about Debbie and the lesson I learned from her so long ago about embracing the greedy girl so she could return my life to balance. Debbie's timeless wisdom lives on in my life.

January 2nd

Today has been a relaxing day. After a morning drive in the snow to get cat food ahead of the big nor'easter that's now hitting the area, Ileen and I came home to watch TV shows and movies. She caught up on *The Good Wife*, while I put together boxes of gifts for Nicole, Terry, Chris, and Robin.

My four-person team takes such good care of my online community and me that I love collecting little presents for them throughout the year to show my appreciation. As I sat on the floor surrounded by gifts, colored tissue paper, boxes, and a bowl full of beautifully wrapped chocolates, I filled each package with goodies, sprinkled candy throughout, and then sprayed the gift cards with balsam fir scent so the boxes would smell like Christmas. Putting these gifts together brings me a surprising amount of joy.

Later on I set up the big computer monitor so we could be warm and cozy by the fire while we watch movies. We just finished *Philomena*, a film about Irish Catholic nuns who took babies from young girls in Ireland and sold them to American couples. It's based on the true story of a woman who, as a young girl living at a convent, was forced to give up her toddler for adoption in the US. She spends the next fifty years searching for her son, only to discover that he'd died of AIDS and had been buried in the same convent he'd been taken from. Turns out he'd been looking for her, too. I wept for families traumatized by these events. Judi Dench (who played Philomena) and Steve Coogan (who played the journalist who helped her) were terrific.

Michael and Ileen are planning to watch another movie together, but instead of joining them, I'm going to take a hot bath with the outdoor deck lights on so I can watch the snow fall while I'm in the tub. I crave warmth, alone time, and beauty. My hip is aching after running yesterday, so a long soak in warm water with salts, baking soda, and essential oils will do me good.

January 5th

We've had a lot of snow this week—more than eighteen inches—and it's been bone cold. This morning I woke up feeling like a caged animal. I stalked through the house from window to window, staring at the massive snowdrifts in the backyard, and all I could think was, *I need freedom, warmth, and green. How many more weeks of this must we endure?*

I made a cup of tea, then went to inspect the backyard further for traces of animals. Yesterday there were tracks all over the field and in and around my garden so I knew the deer were looking for food. I decided to help out by shoveling off a large patch of snow, exposing the grass underneath. After all that work, I was eager to see if the deer had come by to eat. Unfortunately, I didn't find any new tracks.

Staring out over the fields for a while inspired me to go for a walk around the neighborhood. For the first three miles or so, I saw deer tracks everywhere and was lucky enough to see a few cardinals and a couple of red squirrels, too. Bright spots in a desolate landscape. When I circled the reservoir, however, I discovered something upsetting. A doe must have wandered out onto the frozen lake overnight, slipped on the ice, and ended up as dinner for the coyotes I sometimes hear howling at night. While I know all animals need to eat, it broke my heart to find the ravaged carcass of one of my deer out on the ice.

I stood at the water's edge in tears and began to silently pray for her sweet soul. There are not many things that can send me over the edge, but the suffering of an animal will do it every time. I probably inherited this sensitive gene from my mother, who has always had an uncanny connection to animals. As a young girl, I marveled at her ability to communicate with our cats and dogs in an unspoken language that had them following her everywhere. She rarely issued commands. She didn't have to. Instead she talked to our family pets as if they were humans and they responded like loyal friends.

Sometimes it's tough being a person who feels things deeply. It's both a blessing and a curse. On the one hand it's been useful in my work as a coach and teacher. Being perceptive and empathic often lets me know what's really going on with people when they're struggling. I can hear and feel the truth beneath their words. But this sensitivity also causes me a lot of pain, and for some reason this is most true when it comes to animals. The moment I saw the dead deer, I tried to ward off the sinking feeling in the pit of my stomach with strong self-talk. *Pull it together, Cheryl,* I told myself. *You have to stop being so concerned about all the animals in the neighborhood. Other people don't get this upset. Face it, death is just a part of life.*

That's when I saw her. Off in the distance, gradually making her way toward me, was a woman dressed in a long, brown coat and a hood that nearly covered her face. She carried a crumpled paper bag, and periodically she'd stop, reach into the bag, and pull out a handful of what appeared to be birdseed. I watched it scatter on top of the frozen landscape as she tossed the food across the snow-covered field. When she reached me, she smiled, nodded hello, and continued on her way.

As I walked home, I marveled at the mysterious woman who appeared out of nowhere. Although a stranger, I felt oddly comforted by her. *It turns out that my tender heart has company,* I thought, *I'm not the only one concerned about wildlife in our neighborhood. I clear patches of grass, she spreads food.*

Speaking of food, as I sit here finishing this entry, I look up from my laptop and can't believe what I see. A young doe is approaching the patch of grass I cleared yesterday, her dark gray coat in sharp contrast to the fresh white snow. She looks thin, but healthy. As she slowly bends her head to pull at a clump of grass, I stand and walk to the window. I love her gentle face and the fluffy white underside of her tail. Seeing her eat makes me happy. Suddenly her big ears perk up; she lifts her head and turns to look my way. "Hello, sweet one," I say to the doe through the glass. "Hang in there. We'll get through this winter together."

January 7th

The New Year has begun and so has the pressure. New year. New you. New goals. New plans. Ileen left yesterday, signaling the end of the holidays, and now it feels like going back to school after a great summer vacation. The working world swings back into action at the beginning of the year, and now it's time for business. There are travel plans to make, writing to be done, blog posts to be crafted and speeches to be booked. I love what I do, but I have a tendency to adopt an "all work and no play" attitude during this time of year. This is when a witnessing perspective comes in handy. When I remember to step back and watch my thoughts, I notice an old pattern—an underlying belief that I have to get everything done at once, and that I can't stop to enjoy my life in between completing tasks.

I think about May Sarton and how her journals included frequent entries about the torturous struggles of getting to her mail, finishing work in her office, or tending to house projects. She, too, seemed plagued by an inner taskmaster who held peace of mind at bay until duties were done. Well, I refuse to live my life that way, yet sometimes when I feel caught up in it, I can't see a way out. I also wonder if this pressure I put on myself to get things done might have something to do with the discomfort I feel at having more space in my life. I'm sitting with the mystery of not knowing where this winter will take me. *Stay busy*, I tell myself, *get lost in your to-do list, create order, feel more in control.*

I may book a therapy session with Sylvia or call my friend Ellen, whose wisdom I trust and respect. I'm learning to reach out for perspective and healthy mirroring rather than go it alone.

January 9th

This afternoon I drove into Boston to attend a pitch meeting for angel investors—men and women who give of their time, experience, and money to start-up companies that have developed cutting-edge products and services. My interest resurfaced last year after Michael and I invested in Tina and John's company, Visible Good. We loved their idea of building safe and affordable shelter systems that would provide temporary housing during natural disasters. Not long after, I discovered the TV show *Shark Tank*, and my enthusiasm grew further. Not only could angel investing be financially rewarding, but it would also allow me to keep a hand in coaching, something I love and miss. For years I enjoyed working with smart, talented people who were developing good companies, and yet I haven't wanted to go back to it in a formal way. So the thought of becoming an angel investor left me excited at the prospect of giving back by coaching entrepreneurs and CEOs again, but in a more manageable, satisfying way.

No sooner had I set an intention to explore this area further when things started to happen. One afternoon while out for a walk, I said out loud to the Universe, "I'd like to learn more about angel investing and, if it's in my highest and best interest, please give me a sign that I'm meant to move forward." Then I let the thought go. At this point I've learned that the less attached I am to an outcome, the quicker I get into a flow state where synchronicities occur.

That night the first sign appeared. An email showed up from an old friend inviting me to attend a talk on this type of investing. That event led to lunch with an experienced angel investor, which then led to an invitation to join a local angel investor group meeting as a guest. Because I kept feeling enthusiastic about the idea, I kept saying yes, and in a matter of a few weeks, I joined a group. Now I'm investing alongside smart, openhearted businesspeople, and I've started taking classes on everything from term sheets and valuations to leading deals and conducting due diligence.

It feels good to be a student, and the people I've met thus far are intellectually stimulating and fun. So often in the past, I'd be cynical or suspicious of something new and not say yes to life's invitations. But that's changing now, too. I remember one of the regrets I noted on my fiftieth birthday: be less defended and more open to others. I am more open, and a new world is rising up to meet me.

Walking out the door and across the parking lot after today's meeting in downtown Boston, I breathed in the cold, crisp air and stared up at the city skyline. The mirrored windows of the surrounding skyscrapers reflected the setting sun and seagulls floating in the breeze. Jets leaving Logan Airport flew low and loud overhead, but I felt peaceful. It was another moment of being fully present, and I smiled at the realization that I'm relying less on my head to make decisions about my life and more on my emotions and intuition. Things that make me feel alive and excited are now first in line for my attention.

I think back to our London trip last fall, to the inklings I had about what I needed—more time at home and in nature, connection to a local community, new creative ways to express myself—and I'm beginning to see them unfold. Yes, the year of the snake is over, a year of molting, of shedding old beliefs, patterns, relationships, and goals. The year of the horse is under way, and already I'm galloping toward new horizons.

150

January 10th

I've just returned from an intense session with Sylvia. I went to see her to explore the pressure I've been feeling since the New Year to see what might be going on underneath. We talked about my history of being overly responsible, hyper-vigilant, and driven, and how I'm challenging these old patterns. I hadn't planned on doing a regression with Sylvia, but as we talked I felt the familiar energy rise in my body, and I knew the past was calling.

For more than a year now, the past-life regression therapy I've been doing with Sylvia has taught me a great deal about myself. It's been a fascinating process, a very different kind of therapy, and it's been enormously helpful. I'm having the same experience now that I had more than twenty-five years ago when I first tried it after reading Brian Weiss's groundbreaking book *Many Lives, Many Masters*. Brian is an Ivy League-trained psychiatrist who stumbled upon the healing power of recalling past lives while working with a patient, Catherine, who sought his help for anxiety, panic attacks, and phobias. When conventional methods to treat her didn't work, he tried hypnosis. At first she revisited early childhood experiences that seemed to relate to her symptoms, but doing so didn't relieve her distress. Then one day, as Brian continued the regression process, Catherine suddenly began to recall past-life memories that proved to be at the root of her symptoms in this life. Surprised and skeptical, Brian made a decision to trust the process. He continued to guide Catherine through these past-life experiences as her issues began to resolve. Eventually, with each passing session, her symptoms completely disappeared.

I still remember attending Brian's lecture after reading his book. Listening to him talk about the astounding results his clients were experiencing through regression work—from relief from lifelong fears and phobias to overcoming chronic pain—I became fascinated by him and his work. I was so taken by the experience that I volunteered at his workshops so I could participate in the regressions he did with his audiences. I was amazed by how real it felt to be in another lifetime. During the process deep emotions were released, and I often felt cleansed and unburdened afterward.

Back then I was in a relationship with a man that needed to end, but I just couldn't make the break. After doing a regression with a Boston-based therapist Brian recommended, something profound shifted. During the session, I experienced a lifetime in the 1600s when I was married to an abusive man, and after tolerating years of violent beatings, I made the fateful decision to kill him.

In this regression, my husband came home drunk and angry one night, and fearing for my life and the lives of my children, I shot him as he came through the door. I was arrested for his murder, tried, convicted, and sentenced to death by hanging. With the therapist gently guiding me, I experienced my own death during the regression without any fear or pain. After dying and leaving my body, I had a flash of insight. I suddenly understood that I had carried the burden of guilt from that experience into this lifetime.

The same soul in a different body, my husband from way back then was now my boyfriend in this lifetime. Guilt over what I'd done in the past was keeping me tied to this hopeless relationship in the present. After just one session of reliving that centuries-old trauma and coming to terms with my guilt and regret in a new way, my feelings changed. The following week I ended the relationship with my boyfriend for good.

As unfathomable as this kind of therapy seemed to my logical mind back then (and still does sometimes, even now), I've come to focus on the positive ways it continues to affect my life. I thank God that my commitment to personal growth has always been far more important to me than my skepticism. If trying something new or unusual will help me to heal or understand myself on a deeper level, then I'm open and ready to give it a shot. For me, past-life regression therapy has proved to be one of the quickest and most effective ways to shift old patterns and beliefs so I can make different choices in my daily life. That's what drew me back to it this year.

I started my latest regression with Sylvia by closing my eyes, drawing my energy inward, and focusing my attention on a deep, quiet place inside, a place I've visited many times before. Then the process began. I saw darkness, a blackened city destroyed by war. It was an old city, somewhere outside of the US—in Europe, maybe. I was a young woman of thirty with a small child, and I was desperate to find food. As I watched the scene unfold, I suddenly felt a deep grief rise up inside me in present time, and I began to weep, gently at first, but then my body was racked with sobs.

Sylvia encouraged me to ease away from the scene a bit, so I took a few deep breaths and imagined looking down on myself from above. She then asked me to tell her what was going on. "I don't want to go there," I said out loud. I sensed a heavy, dark place that I knew held a lot of pain. I took several more deep breaths, and suddenly I became aware that I'd been searching for food everywhere without luck. Without anyone to turn to for help, my child and I were starving to death in this devastated, war-torn city.

The pain of this realization was overwhelming and I wept brokenly, overcome with guilt and terror at my helplessness and my inability to feed my child, a little girl of just three or four. I felt mired in an endless bog of pain, and I cried for quite some time. I couldn't remove myself from this horror story, so Sylvia suggested I call in spiritual help—higher beings to guide me. I immediately felt the presence of Debbie encouraging me to stay with the darkness in order to understand it and receive the gifts it contained. It was at this point that the conscious part of me kicked in. *I must be making this up*, I thought to myself. *This is nuts.*

But the emotions were real, and deep, and old. Very old. Riddled with guilt and shame for not being able to save my child, I felt part of me was still stuck in that lifetime. The phrase *worthy of punishment* popped into my head, and in that moment I no longer wanted to leave the painful experience behind; being with it felt like performing some sort of penance. I didn't feel worthy of forgiveness, yet at the same time I longed for it. Sylvia gently tried to move me along, but I wouldn't budge. So she let me dwell in that space for a while, until suddenly I felt my awareness expand.

I began to understand several things:

> I came into this lifetime with the belief that I needed to mother others in order to make up for not being a good mother to my little girl.

> Having carried the heavy weight of responsibility from that experience into this life, I've felt the need to take responsibility for others. It will be difficult for me to free myself from this pattern without forgiving myself for what happened.

> Poupon is here to give me the experience of successfully caring for a being that is totally dependent on me. He also offers me the nurturing connection I missed with my child because of the terrible hardships she and I endured.

> I must learn to make my needs more of a priority rather than be run by guilt. The guilty seek punishment, and I no longer need to do penance.

> I now understand why I have such deep empathy for the suffering of animals, and for all living beings. I know why those feelings seem disproportional at times, too.

As Sylvia continued to guide me, I saw my child and myself lying on the side of the road like a bundle of discarded rags, the little girl wrapped in my arms under my coat. We had died together in that spot.

Just writing these words brings back those sharp pangs of loss. During the regression, I had difficulty abandoning those forlorn bodies by the roadside. Some part of me needed to stay, to try to make sense out of my despair. But it was no use. As I looked at the image, I kept repeating, *It makes no sense. It makes no sense. It makes no sense.*

Sylvia asked me once again to call in helpers from a higher realm, and this time Mother Mary appeared, and instantly I felt comforted. She stood above me, dressed all in white, arms outstretched. She gathered me and my child into her arms, and I felt a slight shift in energy away from the darkness. Sylvia asked me to find a place of forgiveness within me, and when I couldn't, she invited me to look into the eyes of one of my helpers and describe what I saw. Debbie stood before me, and in her steady gaze I saw a bottomless well of love and compassion, feelings I know she would have offered me if she were still alive.

I also felt the intense power of the Divine Mother. Her embrace infused me and my daughter with her love, compassion, and forgiveness. Sylvia asked me to meet the spirit of the child, and Mother Mary responded by holding out the light-filled body of my little girl. I knew she was okay, and from a profound place inside myself I greeted the awareness that we were both spirits who shared a lifetime together. We had an experience, and now it was complete.

I wanted to understand why I'd chosen to visit this lifetime and what I was meant to learn from it. The answer came quickly. We are not our physical bodies or our physical existence. We are here to experience all facets of life, and it was time for me to feel what it's like to be a helpless victim. Even the intolerable passes, and the indomitable soul lives on. As I gathered lessons from this lifetime, I allowed the image of the devastated city to fade as Mother Mary and her helpers lifted me up. Sylvia also suggested that I release any remaining ties to the feelings this past life had evoked. I felt my whole body lighten as I followed her gentle voice.

When I finally emerged from the regression, I sat quietly for a long time, allowing myself to integrate the experience. In this higher state, I could feel the sacred nature of my partnership with Sylvia. We are two souls working together to support growth through the transcendence of physical form.

The most meaningful part of our regression work is the way in which it connects me to something bigger than myself. In the expanded state of a regression, I'm able to remember that there is no finite time. We live many lifetimes simultaneously, and each of these lifetimes is intended to advance our mission of growth and healing. I'm able to understand, at a very deep level, the nature of the soul that extends beyond this body and its brief span on earth.

And then there's love. The love that connects us, binds us to one another, and transcends time. It's hard to capture all this in words. A past-life regression needs to be experienced to be understood, but once you travel back in time, you *know* the truth. With each session I leave feeling more empowered, better able to use my voice, unhooked from patterns and people I've allowed to hold me back from living a more authentic version of myself. It doesn't matter whether or not it's real; I know what the work does for me and my life, and I'm deeply grateful for that.

It'll be interesting to see how my life changes after this experience.

January 11th

This morning I'm enjoying a rare view outside the living-room window as I sit here waiting for a friend to visit. The temperature has reached nearly fifty degrees, and as the warm air heats the snow, it releases an iridescent mist that dances with the gusty wind. I've never seen anything like this. It's a treasure. A memory that will carry me through this final stretch of winter darkness.

January 12th

Today I can feel a tiny hint of spring stirring in my body. Outside it's sunny and forty-five degrees. I went for a long walk in the neighborhood early this morning, and then again later at the beach. As I walked along the shore, lulled by the steady roar of crashing waves, I closed my eyes and imagined gliding on a boogie board in the heat of the summer, the way I used to when life was simpler, and I was in the habit of having fun for its own sake. It's good therapy.

These days, as I consider the new, emerging priorities in my life, I continue to be guided by thoughts about death. That sounds dark, I know, but in this case it's not. I'm learning to befriend the part of me that feels the need to keep my mortality on the front burner. When I find myself suffering for too long in order to write a gracious email saying no to a request, or feeling frustrated while lugging last-minute packages to the post office before they close, I ask myself, *Am I doing what I really want to do in this moment? Is this how I want to spend my energy? Can someone else do this so I have more time and space for what matters to me?*

I'm trying to get a fresh perspective, to step back from the routines that define my day in order to see how satisfied I am with the choices I'm making. Our lives are shaped by the actions we take every single day, from the mundane errand or the therapy session to the project we take on at work or the conversations we have with our friends, our partner, or our pets. I want to stay awake. I want to stand witness to the choices I make that sculpt this one precious life. I want to stay connected to who I am today, not reflexively serve the person I've been in the past.

At times like this, thoughts of impermanence are a gift if we're brave enough to entertain them. For most of us, the thought of death is a frequent guest, one who continues to visit despite the fact that we do our best to ignore her. I'm making friends with this visitor because I know she has something vital to teach me. *Stand back,* she says. *Observe your life. Stay tethered to your soul.*

I want my life to be well lived, to be a true expression of my most authentic self. And I must stay awake to do so.

January 14th

There's a gentle rain falling on the metal roof over the living room, and the muffled raindrops sound like a troupe of tap dancers learning a new routine. It's been another misty, gray day with temperatures close to fifty. A warm reprieve in the middle of winter.

I woke this morning at 3:30 a.m. and couldn't get back to sleep. I tried reading, but it didn't help the way it usually does, so I finally got up at 5 a.m. to start my day. I made a cup of tea and sat in the dark living room, eventually falling asleep on top of a heating pad on the couch. My lower back and hips have been sore ever since I started taking longer walks up and down hills, yet I love being outdoors so much I don't want to stop.

It's strange being home for a long stretch of time. One minute I'm happy and at peace, and the next I'm daydreaming about taking a vacation with Michael so I can test-drive the notion of traveling purely for pleasure. When I imagine packing and getting on an airplane, however, I lose steam. Staying put has more appeal. I just need to face the fact that this is a time of transition. I'll question my choices. I'll feel conflicted. And my mood will dance with the wind. It's the old "zone of in between" that I've talked about with students for years—an ambiguous state of being that's never been a favorite of mine. As much as I've wanted this time at home, I'm not used to being so stationary. And I'm not used to being present with the feelings that emerge from stillness, nor am I always a compassionate witness to the unfamiliar voices inside that clamor to be heard.

I feel like I'm in a waiting room, staring at a door I hope will open soon to reveal some insight into what comes next. And, of course, the act of waiting invites the familiar voices of fear to visit. *You're hurting your career,* they tell me. *You're losing ground by not being out there. You'd better get back on the circuit, publish more books, and teach more workshops.*

But I can't. I can't do anything but inhabit the space I'm in right now. I'm resting, emptying myself. I have to let go of what no longer works without knowing what will, and I have no idea how long it will take to shed this old identity. Today, when being in limbo became too uncomfortable, I called my friend Ellen to talk about what was going on. She's a wise and loving coach whose advice I cherish and trust. After listening to me describe feeling adrift and unable to figure out what's next, she said one simple thing that made a huge difference.

"Your meandering has purpose."

No sooner were the words out of her mouth than I felt my whole body relax. This time of healing and renewal is justified, she reminds me. Living in limbo is necessary.

I'm so glad I reached out for help. It was wonderful to be on the receiving end of such elegant coaching. Ellen's deep listening allowed her to formulate one simple line that would instantly shift my consciousness. The idea of meandering being purposeful appealed both to the artist in me who craves the space to wander, and imagine, and create; and to the CEO who demands a productive form of action.

Coaching that causes an internal shift that changes the way we see the world is coaching at the highest level. Bless you, dear Ellen.

162

January 15th

I woke early this morning to watch golden light spilling over the wintry field outside my window. One by one, the trees came to life, bathed by the sun's magnificence. I'm awestruck by nature. It humbles me and renders me speechless. What would it be like if I allowed myself to live in this world devoid of technology—computers, cell phones, and social media? I imagine sinking comfortably into the present moment to write and rest, daydream and be. That space for contemplation seems to be constantly slipping away in my modern life. I can feel it elude me. And I'm grasping to hold on.

January 16th

This morning I had a beautiful dream.

I'm somewhere in Europe, driving down a country road, when I come across a small village. I stop to explore, and I meet a young, handsome man with long, dark hair. He seems strong yet tender, sensual in an understated way, his masculine and feminine aspects well balanced. We talk for a bit and decide to take a train together to a nearby city. I'm hypnotized by his warm, magnetic brown eyes.

While sitting on the train, I notice him move his left arm awkwardly and wince with pain. It turns out he injured it, and I can tell he has been struggling to hide how much it hurts. I gently lean over and kiss his shoulder as if to ease the pain. He smiles. Now and then we look at each other, knowing there's something between us.

Before understanding dream work, I would have thought this to be a romantic dream about another man, but today I know that the people who show up in my dreams usually represent aspects of myself that are trying to get my attention.

The energy of this dream is soft and gentle, yet haunting. This man—tender and strong—is similar to men I've met in dreams before. He represents a new kind of masculinity, one that's balanced by a more feminine presence. His injured left arm may be related to the fact that my shoulders and arms have been bothering me, but it may also represent the left-brain, more masculine way of thinking and acting, the well-developed side of me that may need permission to rest and heal. I wake with a sense that there's something more to be learned about the power of presence and sensuality, and the need for more of a partnership between my inner male and female.

January 20th

I enjoyed a good night's sleep with Michael last night and woke feeling happy. Michael was awake, and we both said, "Look at that sunrise" at exactly the same time. We laughed and watched the sun come up together. Poupon was sound asleep between us, peaceful and content.

I had a very productive morning, too. I'm using a time management method my sister Kerri shared with me called the "Pomodoro Technique," named by its inventor, Francesco Cirillo, a university student who used a tomato-shaped kitchen timer to remind him to take frequent breaks while doing schoolwork. (*Pomodoro* is the Italian word for tomato.)

While using the technique, I set an alarm for 25 minutes and work intently. Then I stop for a break when the alarm goes off. I'd only been doing this for a couple of days when I noticed something interesting. The rebellious kid in me who doesn't want to be forced to work calms down. She retreats and allows me to focus and complete things I keep putting off, like responding to email or finishing descriptions of the talks I need to give next year.

This afternoon, feeling satisfied with the amount of work I accomplished, I put on my new snowshoes and went for a hike through the fields out back. I trudged up and down hills, investigating the woodsy places where deer hide in the winter, and enjoyed the snowy silence of dusk. Before finishing my adventure and heading in to the house, I tamped down a giant heart in the snow just outside the bathroom window so Michael would see it when he takes a shower. When I looked out tonight, the heart glowed in the moonlight.

I smiled, and the heart smiled back.

January 21st

Another good night of sleep, and I wake feeling content and happy—a wonderful way to start the day. This morning I need to finish a few writing projects, including an article for a website and descriptions of next year's events. These are tasks only I can perform, and I find it frustrating that they take me away from this journal—the writing that means the most to me right now.

It's the tension between worlds. In one I engage with others as a teacher, and I advocate for my work. In the other I conserve my energy as if putting the lid on a pot of boiling water, trying my best to generate creative steam. These days, because I'm partial to the inner world, I thank God for the discipline I've developed over the last fifteen years while writing weekly newsletters. This practice has taught me to keep a foot in each world, fulfilling the needs of both.

This afternoon there's more snow coming, and I'm happy for the chance to use my new snowshoes again. It's funny how one purchase can change the entire experience of winter. These awkward attachments give me a new access to nature, and encourage me to continue to move my body every day. Developing the discipline to get outside has made an enormous difference to my physical *and* emotional health. I want to exercise now. I want to take in crisp, fresh air. I want to be immersed in a hushed landscape of hills and trees and birds and deer. I want a front-row seat to enjoy the season as it unfolds before me.

January 23rd

It's been gray the last two days, and bitterly cold. We were supposed to have a big storm on Tuesday night, but it moved out to sea. I slept next to Michael and woke at sunrise, and when I got up to use the bathroom, I looked at the outside thermometer. It was only three degrees Fahrenheit. So I stayed in bed longer than I normally would, cuddling with Michael and Poupon. It's hard to leave a warm bed in the dead of winter.

Yesterday I drove down to have lunch with Dad. While I'm not always enthusiastic about the three hours it takes to get there and back, I feel fortunate that Michael and I still have our parents with us. Most of our friends have lost one if not both of theirs, so we stay connected as often as we can.

I usually make it a monthly ritual to see Dad for lunch, but I missed last month and could tell he was especially happy to see me this time. I feel for him because he's a sociable man with a sharp mind, but his activities have been limited by his hearing loss and ill health. He can't move around like he used to, and he's not as stimulated socially as he'd like to be. He's fond of reminding me that many of his friends have passed on, not in a morose way, but as a matter of fact, like this is how it is. He's lonely, and although Mom keeps him company, he longs for the days when he was working and able to be out and about town interacting with people.

Dad and I went to a local Italian restaurant, and he stayed true to his ritual of pulling out a large envelope with treasures for us to discuss—a couple of thank-you cards he received from the homeless organization he supports, a funny email about the elderly coping with technology, and a few pages of back exercises with the most helpful ones highlighted for me to pass on to Michael's dad, who's struggling with a back injury. My dad is a very thoughtful man.

He also took out a picture of members of the Elks lodge he belonged to for many years. I recognized some faces but couldn't put names to them, so Dad went over each one, reminding me who they were and sharing stories about them and their families. I'm always struck by Dad's remarkable memory for details going way, way back. I don't think he gets the credit he deserves for his bright mind. I must tell him how much I appreciate it.

I visited with Mom when Dad and I returned from lunch, her blue eyes smiling into mine as she and I caught up on the details of her life. Her eyes reminded me of our trip to Baltimore together. We were standing outside the hotel waiting for the car that would take us to an event I was doing with Oprah Winfrey when a man walked right up to my mother and said, "Medusa eyes." Mom and I looked at each other and then back at him, stunned by the suddenness of his approach. Hypnotized by her baby blues, he stood there staring for what seemed like several minutes before walking away.

Medusa eyes, indeed.

I left my parents' house feeling happy I'd made the trip down to visit. I wish they lived closer so I could just drop in now and then. We're entering into a new, tender stage in our relationship, where I suspect they'll need more care and I'll have a chance to learn how to walk the fine line between honoring their independence and offering support. I'm uncomfortable with entertaining the notion that our parents become our children as they age. Both Mom and Dad are far too emotionally independent—actually *anti*dependent—for me to even allow that thought to enter my mind, let alone suggest anything like it. I don't suspect it will be an easy road, but it is one that must be traveled.

January 27th

I just finished watching a video about an extraordinary animal communicator named Anna Breytenbach from South Africa. Hollie emailed me a clip of the work Anna did with a black leopard named Diablo who had been moved to a wildlife sanctuary after being imprisoned in a small cage. Anna was brought in to communicate with Diablo, to find out what he needed in order to feel safe and comfortable in his new home. Among the requests she received from him was that his name be changed, so now he's known as Spirit.

As I watched Anna's story unfold, it touched that deep place within me that feels a kinship with wildlife, a passion to protect all beings, and a longing to return to the sanctity of the natural world. I fear we're losing sight of our responsibilities as stewards of this planet, and it's heartbreaking. There's too much destruction, too little regard for the environment that supports all living beings.

Greed trumps common sense and tramples the sacred.

As I type these words, I can hear owls hooting to each other outside my bedroom window, and I imagine they're tuning in to my thoughts. We need to reconnect with the miracle of life on our planet, because we're running out of time.

January 29th

I've been rereading this journal, making small changes to improve its flow. It's a challenge to record your personal thoughts and feelings knowing that someone will read these words later on. I can't help feeling self-conscious.

Speaking of personal thoughts and feelings, today has been a strange day, and I'm feeling more vulnerable than usual. Michael and I had a fight this week, and it wasn't pretty. We went out for dinner on Saturday night, and during the meal, he suggested a new project for the house. Before the words had even finished leaving his mouth, I could feel resentment rising at the thought of managing another project, so I cut him off. "That's a foolish idea," I sniped, resentment mixing with a contemptuous tone, and that's all it took. Michael's buttons got pushed and our date night immediately took a bad turn.

Angry words.

Silent stewing.

More angry words.

An abrupt end to dinner.

A chilly, silent ride home.

Doors slamming.

Separate rooms.

No conversation for three days.

Three days.

As much as I dislike the stress of unspoken anger, three days of silence represents growth for me. In the past I would have done everything in my power to resolve the conflict as soon as possible, so we could return to a state of domestic tranquility. But not anymore. Like Michael, I've learned to sit with uncomfortable feelings, to soothe myself during an emotional crisis, and to take the time and space I need to process the experience. This way I can get clear about my part in creating the mess and what needs to change to make our marriage stronger.

But I do hate fighting, and there are few things that drill an anxious hole in my stomach like conflict with Michael. I have to admit that these days the hostilities are often instigated by me. In my menopausal years, I've come into my own in surprising ways, and it seems I've also lost a filter or two. As a result, pent-up anger from unspoken and unmet needs comes rushing in before I have a chance to close my mouth and the result isn't pretty.

Nastiness is toxic. It leads to defensiveness and withdrawal. And at that point, there's no communication. None at all. Someone needs to write a new owner's manual for the 21st-century woman, a handbook that includes how to ask for what you want when you want it, not weeks, months, or years after the fact. Too often those delays mean the request will come wrapped in a bitter tone that leads to relationship hell.

When I said to Michael, "That's a foolish idea," my tone was harsh and dismissive. That's what happens when you sit on a pile of unexpressed needs because you want to keep the peace, because you want to avoid arguments that go nowhere, or because you're afraid you'll have to work too damn hard to get your needs met in the relationship so you just do everything yourself.

What I really wanted to scream (at the top of my lungs in the middle of the restaurant) was this:

Sure, it's easy for you to have new ideas; you don't have to do all the shit that I do!

I don't want another house project to manage because I'm sick of all the things I already manage!

I'm tired of being the one in charge of everything!

I don't want to carry this load of resentment anymore. I want to drop it right here, right now, in the middle of this damn restaurant!

Oh, and by the way, I'd like a little acknowledgment and appreciation for all that I do!

And have done!

For years!

And while I seem like I'm pissed at you, the truth is I'm furious with myself because I sound like a martyr and a victim, and I know it's my own damn fault.

I suck at getting my needs met.

So there!

God, I hate to admit this. I teach people how to get their needs met, for crying out loud. And the truth is, I know better. I know I have to speak up. I know I have to give voice to what I need, when I need it. And I know that I have to be willing to do what it takes to make sure my needs get met. But at discouraging times like this, I try to remember that as women we haven't had the right to vote for very long, and for thousands of years before that we've had to imprison ourselves in silence in order to stay safe. But that's not the world we live in anymore, and now the very thing we want most—true partnership that is balanced and loving, sexy and supportive, romantic and fun—requires us to speak up.

I also have to remember that growth isn't linear and that we all regress when under pressure. Beating myself up never works. I want to be gentle and forgiving with my humanness.

When the three days had passed and Michael and I finally made peace, we agreed that it was time to put an end to a pattern that wreaks havoc in our relationship. I need to stop holding things inside, and he needs to listen for—and respond to—my needs. Before we schedule date nights, we need to schedule household nights, where we meet on a level playing field every week to negotiate the work that needs to be done together. And we need to send our inner children out to play so they don't make a mess.

While I'd rather not fight, the truth is that conflict is unavoidable when you share a home and a life with someone. There are no shortcuts when it comes to making relationships work, but fortunately there are benefits. Each resolved clash brings a gift in the form of an insight, a memory to draw on, or just the sheer joy of making up.

February 1st

It has been a glorious day. Today was sunny, just above forty degrees, and I was finally able to get out after being cooped up for too long. Now that I've been working out every day, my body is even more insistent about its need for fresh air, sunlight, and time in nature. When I don't get that, I feel depressed and irritable.

Michael and I have been advancing the conversation about how we live and work in partnership. We've been together more than twenty years, and because we're both growing and changing, we can't keep doing things the way we always have. Once again I'm reminded that marriage is deeply satisfying but also hard work. I love my life with Michael, and I appreciate the fact that he shares my passion for living an evolving, conscious life. I also recognize our differences, which provide us with both pitfalls and opportunities for spiritual and psychological growth.

I have to remember that the things that drive me crazy about Michael are often the things I need to focus on within myself. Michael is slower paced and methodical; I often move quickly and deal with the fallout from snap decisions. He's more of an introvert, spending long periods of time alone; I'm more extroverted, although I also tend to complain about my calendar being too full. Michael protects his health and sensitivity by resting, taking breaks, and making conscious transitions between activities; and I'm more spontaneous, and more inclined to say yes when my self-care would benefit from saying no.

Rather than fight, we need to use our differences to make us stronger individually and together.

February 2nd

I spent the whole day today working on a blog post about the fight I had with Michael. I needed to go back and process the experience, and writing about it helps me do that. The end result was not only a piece of writing I felt good about, but also a helpful perspective on the event. When I finished I brought the piece to Michael to read. As I waited, I found myself feeling a little anxious about his reaction. I am, after all, publicly airing the intimate details of our marriage.

His response reminded me of one of the many reasons I love him. He was lying in bed listening while I read it to him, facing away from me so I couldn't see his reactions. When I finished he was quiet for a minute or so (while I squirmed), and then he said, "You have a great way of capturing an experience and telling a story, and some of these lines are just beautiful. I think it's great."

Michael is a truth seeker first and foremost, and a fellow writer who's willing to sacrifice some of his privacy for art and honesty. We talked about changing a few words, but otherwise he appreciated seeing the story in the context of a search for closeness and growth. As I listened to his comments, tears filled my eyes. With all the positive feedback and accolades I receive from being in the public eye, it's his response that means the most.

February 5th

Happy Birthday, Mom!

We're in the throes of yet another blizzard, and I can barely see the water below. When it snows like this, the birch trees in the backyard all but disappear against the opaque sky. If the snow lets up a bit, I may go out to snowshoe before it gets too dark. Which reminds me, I want to check online to see when we change the clocks for daylight savings time. It's usually around this time of year that I get a little lift from knowing more light is on the way.

Let's hope so. I'm going to check now . . .

Wow! The clocks move forward on March 9th, just a few days after I return from my next retreat. For some reason I thought it wasn't until the end of March, so I'm feeling a bit giddy. Only one more month before the days grow noticeably longer and brighter!

I've set my laptop on pillows piled next to me on the love seat. I'm perched in front of the big picture window in the living room, so I have a full view of the snowy reservoir. A small space heater is humming in the background, adding extra warmth to the room, and I have a mint-green smoothie on the coffee table next to me. Today I mixed banana with handfuls of spinach, Vitamineral Green powder, coconut water, almond milk, and some dried peppermint from last year's garden. I attempted to share it with Poupon, but he turned up his little heart-shaped nose and walked away. I forgot that cats don't like peppermint. Wrapped in a warm blanket, I shiver when I look outside at the snow. When it looks cold, I feel cold.

After writing I'm committed to getting my inbox emptied and my desk cleared. It's a big promise I've made to myself, considering that I'd rather lounge around and read or nap. But the weight of this unfinished business feels like a lead vest and I need to get it off. Once again I think of May Sarton and the number of pages she devoted to the angst she felt about responding to letters and getting her desk cleared. I feel for her, and I'd like to handle that challenge differently.

Later

Just got back from snowshoeing through the fields surrounding the house. The barren tree branches created lacy black patterns against an iron sky, and nuthatches darted from branch to branch, leading the way as I trudged along the edge of the woods. I stopped at one point on the crest of the hill and looked back at the wintry wonderland behind me. *I'm so grateful to be here*, I thought to myself. This place provides me with so much beauty and a home to the animals, plants, and birds I adore. Yes, this land invites my love, and it's why I feel such a strong urge to protect it.

February 8th

Mom and her best friend, Theresa, left yesterday after having paid us an overnight visit. Occasionally I'm able to get them here to enjoy a "Queen for a Day" mini vacation, when I like to give them the royal treatment. Mom is reluctant to leave Dad alone these days because of his poor health, but thanks to my sisters who helped out, she was able make this trip.

I turned the library into a spa and arranged for a massage therapist to give Theresa her first massage ever, and

Mom her first one in a long, long time. I moved the big recliner chairs off to the side and set up the massage table in the middle of the room. I covered it with soft, flannel sheets warmed by a toasty heating pad, sprinkled some lavender and geranium essential oils on an eye pillow, and turned the lights down low. Mom told Emmy, the massage therapist, that after Emmy finished with her, Emmy could tell me what my body was going to look like in twenty years. We all had a good laugh.

When their massages were finished, Mom and Theresa were floating on air. I find few things more satisfying than providing people I love with pampering. Later that night, Michael joined us at a local restaurant for lobster dinner, Mom's favorite meal. I was planning to order food from a nearby seafood store to enjoy here at home, but while we were having a glass of wine, the lights went out. I think it was the Universe protecting me from having to clean up a huge mess!

We had quite the feast, too much wine, and so many laughs my stomach hurt. Theresa made homemade apple pie for dessert, which we ate after coming home. I'm still kicking myself for casually asking if the crust was store bought before I took my first bite. In Theresa's world, store-bought crust doesn't exist. The pie begged for a second helping, and we happily answered its call. Full and happy, we all went to bed.

The next day we lounged around, enjoying a light lunch of baked sweet potatoes stuffed with cheddar cheese and spinach, and talked about how a woman's life today is different from the way it was when Mom and Theresa were younger. Both women shared stories about preserving food in an icebox, using a wringer washing machine, and the importance of ironing cloth diapers after hanging them out to dry in the cold air. I had no idea how hard they worked in the "good old days."

Listening to their stories, I felt an enhanced appreciation for the advantages I have today, and for the women who helped build the foundation upon which my life now rests. Women of my generation need to know more about how our ancestors emotionally and physically muscled through a challenging life. It's certainly an eye-opener for me.

We enjoyed two wonderful days together, and as Mom and Theresa were leaving, I closed the front door and said a silent prayer, asking God to guide them home safely. Tears welled up in my eyes as I thought about an exchange between Mom and me about getting older and the limited time we have left together. My first response was to tell her we have plenty of time—a typical default reaction intended to keep the conversation on safe ground—but Mom wouldn't have it. "Cheryl," she said with a hint of steel in her voice, "we don't know how long we have, and I want to tell the truth about that."

A truth we all do our best to ignore.

What I didn't tell my mother is that I've been thinking about death a lot lately. I think about it as I watch her walk down the steps toward the car. I think about it when she calls to sing happy birthday with my dad and then sings another version from her two cats, meowing at the top of her lungs. I think about it with every thank-you card I receive from her in the mail, its passages underlined over and over again to emphasize the message. And I think about it when my mother tells me stories about her life, because I know that someday these stories will slip through the cracks of time, and I'll miss them for the rest of my days.

Today I bow to my mother, an inner acknowledgment of her courage and strength, of the sacrifices she's made and the wisdom she's gleaned from years of making the care of others her biggest priority.

Stay awake, I remind myself nearly every day now. *Be present. Be present.*

February 11th

It's been a strange couple of days. Yesterday I woke and thought, *I just don't want to be a grown-up today.* I resisted going into my office, answering email, going through my to-do pile. I ended up taking a spinning class with my sister Kerri at the end of the day, and it was a wise decision. I worked my ass off on that bike and felt much better afterward. I think part of the problem is that I haven't been going to bed early enough or sleeping straight through. Either Poupon gets in bed next to me and pushes me aside, or he howls at four or five in the morning because he wants to eat.

I crave silence, and although I've been trying to sleep next to Michael again, I've decided to move back in to the guest room to see if it helps. Last night Poupon woke me up at 4:30 and again at 5:30, the little stinker. Sometimes he hears Michael get up and leaps off the bed to go down to see him. Our little cat triggers two strong feelings in me: overwhelming love and frustration. Of course love wins out. I never lock him out of the room, although I sometimes wish I could.

This morning I had a long chat with Joan Borysenko. She's been such a dear friend, and it's been forever since we've talked. I happened to see on Facebook that she was in Boston giving a speech, so I called about getting together. While we couldn't make it work, we did spend an hour on the phone catching up. Joanie is a doll, a beautiful soul who is exceptionally bright, generous, and warm, warm, warm. I love her so much.

We talked about losing Debbie Ford and Candace Pert, the renowned neuroscientist, in the same year. I remember the first time I met Candace. She had recently published *Molecules of Emotion*, and we were both speaking at a conference in Texas. I was in the elevator on the way to my floor when the doors opened and before me stood a round woman with a big floppy hat and wild, colorful clothes. She took one look at me, pointed, and at the top of her lungs yelled, "*You!*"

All of us in the elevator took a collective step backward. "I've been looking for you!" she bellowed, eyes narrowing in on mine. "I need help getting my life in order, and I'm coming to your workshop."

Candace got on the elevator and introduced herself. She said she desperately needed to eliminate the clutter in her life, and I assured her that would be one of the topics in my workshop. We laughed our way up to our respective floors, and sure enough, she attended my talk later that afternoon. We ended up having dinner that night, and I was bowled over by her wit and wisdom. In between answering my questions about peptides, neurotransmitters, and the mind-body connection, Candace told one funny story after another, and both of us roared with laughter. I thought of her recently when I heard about a peptide treatment for HIV. Candace was working on bringing to market Peptide T, a potent HIV drug she had discovered more than twenty years prior.

The light of the world dimmed when Debbie and Candace left the planet, which reminded Joanie and me why it's so important to make time to get together. We've committed to see each other this summer when she's back east, if not sooner. Life is so unpredictable, but I plan to make that get-together happen one way or another.

One of the hardest things about having a busy travel schedule and living in a small country town is that important relationships wind up being virtual instead of in person. I wish I could pick up the phone and invite someone to dinner or tea. There's only so much intimacy to be had via Skype or on the phone, and I much prefer to see the people I love face-to-face. I worry sometimes that the ease and efficiency of technology is not bringing us closer but driving a wedge between us, creating islands where we need bridges.

February 13th

Another snowstorm here today. It started early, around 7 a.m., and it has continued all day. The wind is howling, the snow piling up in massive drifts, and I feel like we're living at the North Pole!

Ileen is visiting, and we've been enjoying our favorite activity: watching movies. We saw *August: Osage County*, which was profoundly depressing. It featured some great acting, though. Meryl Streep plays the pill-popping matriarch of a dysfunctional family, whose interactions were both fascinating and painful to watch. We then watched *Labor Day*, which also featured fine performances, but we fast-forwarded through some of Kate Winslet's convincing portrayal of anxiety and depression in search of a happier ending.

Finally we watched *The Secret Life of Walter Mitty* with Michael. I'd already seen it, but I really wanted to watch it again with him because I knew he'd love it. And he did. I can't remember the last time I've heard him laugh so much. I told him I'd like to visit Iceland, where part of the movie was filmed, and he responded, "Well, if you really want to do it, let's go."

That's another thing I love about Michael—he's up for pretty much anything.

February 21st

I can't believe that eight days have passed since I've written in this journal. Ileen visited for a week, immediately followed by Dad, and it has taken me this long to get back into my routine.

Dad came to stay with us for two days while undergoing cataract surgery in Boston. The procedure had the potential to be tricky because he needed to put it off while handling other health issues, and his cataract had hardened. Possible complications included blindness.

I'd made arrangements with one of the best doctors in Boston, a man who performed the same surgery on a friend and another family member, and having been through this process with them, I volunteered to take Dad through the experience. The staff was wonderful, letting me stay in pre-op right up until Dad went into the surgical suite. He's nearly deaf now, and I needed to communicate on his behalf, otherwise this would have been even more stressful for him. Even with me there, I could tell that he was scared, and understandably so.

I thought of Michael while Dad and I were waiting for the anesthesiologist to administer the first sedative. Michael has a beautiful way of bringing lightness and humor to situations where fear might otherwise rule. I teased my dad about not being able to wear makeup for a couple of weeks, and his need to give up bodybuilding until he was fully recovered. It was my best attempt to evoke Michael's presence since they only allowed one of us to accompany Dad through surgery.

Standing by Dad's bed in pre-op, I could see his anxiety reflected in his elevated heart rate, announced by a beeping monitor. So I kept assuring him he'd be fine. Every time someone on the medical team adjusted his IV, or put drops in his eyes, or wrapped a blood-pressure cuff around his arm, I told Dad everything was going to be okay. At first the beeping didn't slow much. But when I started using a coaching technique known as "you messages," his heart rate came right down to sixty beats per minute. I said things like, "You're doing great, Dad. Your body is responding so well. You're resilient and strong," and it worked beautifully.

When I watched the nurses wheel my father into the operating room, I thought about how remarkable it was to have just seen the mind-body connection work its magic right before my eyes.

Being with Dad for two days was a complicated experience that evoked mixed emotions—sadness, frustration, and plenty of fear. At seventy-nine, he's not in the best of health, and because he's set in his ways, I need to follow his lead. He moves slowly, can barely hear, and gets short of breath when walking, so it required patience and tenderness. I'm so grateful for the chance to spend this time together, even if it is while he's recovering from surgery, as every day feels like a gift.

February 23rd

Yesterday was sunny and fifty degrees, so I spent the afternoon walking on the beach at Plum Island with Kerri and Missy. I was desperate to soak up the sunlight given the relentless string of snowstorms we've endured over the last several weeks.

I checked in with Dad yesterday. He's doing well, and he was excited to tell me that he mastered the technique for putting in eye drops on his own when Mom isn't around to help him. He also thanked me for a "moving experience" over the two days, saying that he felt so well taken care of. Funny, I felt like I hadn't done enough. The older he and Mom get, the more I want to make life special for them, which can create such pressure sometimes. Dad's gratitude for my efforts serves as a good reminder to chill out. They feel cared for.

It's a gray day today, but I see hopeful signs of spring. I saw a robin take off from the interior of the evergreen tree near the front door, which may mean he's scoping out a new home. I've also seen buds forming on the yellow magnolia by the garage, and several more birds flying in and out of spaces underneath the back deck. More house hunting, I imagine. Life is energy, and the more present I can be, the more connected I feel to the flow of it all.

February 24th

I woke up this morning feeling anxious, and I'm not sure what's triggering this feeling of unease. It might be that Michael and I are traveling to Arizona this weekend to teach with Alanis (Morissette), or that Poupon is acting strangely. He's not coming into the kitchen or jumping up on the island for treats, which is normally his favorite activity. He's been acting this way ever since Ileen had a business meeting here with a woman who said she didn't like cats. The woman walked into the kitchen near where Poupon eats, and he came running in to check her out. I noticed that she seemed pretty disinterested, so I asked how she felt about cats. She quickly let me know they were not her favorite animals.

While some people might think it's crazy to make this connection, I have no doubt that Poupon picked up her negative vibe, and it may be why he's avoiding the kitchen. Either way, I'm trying to relax about his behavior, but it's not easy given that I'm going away. I know this little guy, and I can tell he's spooked. We'll be leaving him with a new house sitter because Robin is coming with me, and I'm concerned now that things don't seem right. Perhaps Poupon is just picking up on *my* anxiety. Animals are such energetic mirrors, after all.

It has been a while since I've traveled, and I know that's partly fueling my nervousness. On the one hand, I'm looking forward to warmth and sunshine and teaching with Michael and Alanis. The Miraval retreats are among my favorite events. On the other hand, I've been home for so long that I've become comfortably rooted in my routine, and I don't want to disrupt it. And of course I'll miss our little furry boy.

February 26th

I got more sleep than usual last night, even though it was broken up, and I feel rested. I went to get my hair colored this morning, and it's a relief to finally have it done. If there's one thing that really frustrates me about aging, it's having to dye my hair. Now that my roots are turning mostly gray, I could really stand to do it once a month, and yet I don't want to put chemicals on my head that frequently. At all, actually. So this time I waited almost two months, using a color stick to get me through, and by the time I reached the salon this morning, I was desperate to get cleaned up. I'm not ready to become a gray girl just yet, but I can see that day coming.

February 28th

I'm still feeling anxious about leaving. There are so many details to manage before an event—logistics, packing, and planning. This morning, in an effort to put my worried mind at ease, I asked myself: *Do you want to cancel? Is it even possible to cancel?* Once I knew the answer was no, I told myself that I have no choice but to stop ruminating about reality. It's a little trick I've started using. No more fretting about what I can't change. If I put my energy into worrying, I'll just find more and more things to worry about. Instead, I choose to put my energy into ease and peace.

Today I have to remember to stay in charge of my thoughts. When I get all twitchy about whatever is happening, I need to tell myself:

Cheryl, be present.

Remember who you are: a soul in a physical body.

Don't scare yourself with your thoughts.

Choose better ones.

Okay, I'm off to get a few things done in preparation for the trip. First up is to create instructions that spell out how to care for Poupon. My new assistant, Kim, will be staying here while we're gone, and I want to cover exactly what he needs in great detail. Of course, I know this list is more for my benefit than hers. Kim is wonderful with animals and knows what to do. I'm sure Poupon will love her.

March 1st

I'm sitting on a plane bound for Phoenix, a direct flight that will end with a car ride to Tucson for the retreat. I'm happy to be heading toward warm weather and sun, especially since the forecast for this part of Massachusetts calls for more snow.

I've decided to end this journal on the first day of spring, a time of endings and new beginnings, and as we near that date, I'm contemplating the themes that have shown up in my life thus far. Sometimes I still feel like I'm living in limbo. I'm used to focusing on the pursuit of something, and this emphasis on staying in place, in the mystery, leaves me feeling unmoored. It's a helpful spiritual practice, though, to love and accept these feelings (and myself) as they arise. *Hang on, kiddo,* I tell myself. *A new version of your life is being programmed, and if you stay true to this process and have faith, you'll be pleased with the upgrade.*

Right now I need to train my sights on teaching. Because Miraval is a weeklong retreat, I'm able to go deeper with people, which makes it the most satisfying of all my events. I love the challenge of working on an individual problem and finding a way to make the resolution relevant (and helpful) to everyone in the room. I also appreciate the chance to use some of my favorite tools, like EFT (the Emotional Freedom Technique, also known as the tapping technique). Working with the body's energy system and tapping on the same points used in acupuncture for thousands of years, I'm able to gain access to intuitive information that lets me know exactly where to go to help someone get unstuck. The more energy work I do, the more I find it to be an elegant and efficient method for healing, and I suspect it will play a more prominent role in my work moving forward.

March 2nd

I'm sitting on the veranda looking out over the snow-capped Santa Catalina Mountains, a view I've enjoyed for more than fifteen years while coming to Miraval. The early sun gently bathes the hills, brush, and occasional saguaro cactus with its diffuse light, and the smell of sage hangs heavy in the air.

Before going to bed last night, I heard a pack of coyotes howling in the distance, which took me right back to my first visit here. Back then I was nervous and excited to be teaching my first retreat, and Tucson felt like an exotic foreign land. I was lying in bed encouraging my body to relax, when a cacophony of barks and yowls brought me to my feet. Amplified by the surrounding hills, the mournful coyote symphony sounded like it was taking place right outside my window. I wasn't scared; I was fascinated by animal sounds I'd never heard before. The memory still makes me smile.

It's funny how life keeps circling around again and again.

I enjoyed breakfast with my friend Robin, who's assisting me on this trip. We visited the buffet and filled our bowls with steel-cut oatmeal and gorgeous blueberries, blackberries, and raspberries. I also ordered a small egg-white veggie omelet, and it felt like the perfect way to start the day. My soul is happy here. I'm sure it will be a full and gratifying week.

March 3rd

Our Self-Care for the Creative Soul retreat is going well. Yesterday Michael, Alanis, and I shared the stage, and the dance between us unfolded beautifully. It was interesting to see Michael providing calm, nurturing, arguably feminine energy, as he sat between two strong alpha women. Alanis is electric and bright. Deep wisdom flows from her in a river of poetry. She has a unique teaching style. Like a raptor circling its prey, she begins her teaching from the highest perspective and spirals down, down, down to the simplest and purest form of truth. Michael is thoughtful, intuitive, and slower paced, like a gentle rain that doesn't run off but seeps into the consciousness of the audience. More than a few people have commented on how much they're enjoying his loving, compassionate energy.

For my part, I've taken on the role of conductor, doing my best to skillfully orchestrate the music that's being made between us and the audience.

March 4th

This morning I'm disoriented in the most delightful way. I'm so used to seeing Michael in his role as my husband that it's a treat to see him as a teacher interacting with the audience. He did a wonderful job last night speaking about what it was like growing up as a sensitive, creative man. I listened as he described being bullied, and his subsequent decision to physically "armor up" by working out at the gym. And then how he realized the cost of that decision years later, living through two major bouts of depression before recognizing the need to slowly dismantle the protective walls he'd also built around his heart.

I watched him give advice to a woman with a sensitive son, encouraging her to support her boy with deep listening and consistent acknowledgment that his experience is valid. Michael was relaxed, openhearted, and self-effacing in the most attractive way. Seeing him in action, I wondered if we might teach together more in the future. Maybe a relationship workshop where we share some of the deliberate and conscious ways we're rewriting outdated tribal rules, and making our partnership stronger. It's just an inkling at this point, another glimpse into what may come. We'll see . . .

March 5th

I'm lying on the deck off of my room looking out at the spacious blue sky and a lone hawk making lazy circles overhead. I can feel my body melting into the chaise lounge, relaxing in the dry desert heat.

This morning I had a difficult conversation with an attendee. She was angry with me, and as fate would have it, we ran into each other on the path to the dining room. When I teach here at Miraval, I think of the paths around the property as magical byways where I connect with participants who need a bit of additional support—an encouraging word, a hug, or a "get something off my chest" conversation. In this case I listened to the woman's complaints and did my best to not get triggered.

She explained that she wasn't getting some of her needs met, and when she suggested that she wasn't the only one, I stopped her as I always do when someone pulls the "and I'm not the only one" card. I requested that she please speak from her own direct experience. To her credit she stopped herself,

196

and simply gave voice to her own unhappiness. She explained that last night I had cut her off during a Q&A period in an effort to stay on track and manage time. She felt I did so in an abrupt way, and made the decision that I didn't like her. She was testy and abrupt herself, and in that moment, feeling slapped by the anger she'd been stoking overnight, I *didn't* like her. So I had to work hard to manage my own reaction while continuing to listen.

This is the unseen work of a teacher who deals with the public and wants to be sure that her offerings come from a place of integrity. While there's much to be done in my outer world—travel, speech and workshop development, the actual presenting, writing books, coaching, etc., all of which requires enormous focus, discipline, and energy—the inner work is equally taxing, if not more so. When I have an exchange with a student who pushes my buttons, I lean back on the years I've invested in my own therapy and coaching, the hours spent reading hundreds of personal development books and attending workshops and trainings myself, to try to handle it well. It's important to me that my unhealed or unfinished stuff doesn't get in the way of supporting the autonomous growth of my students.

Fortunately I was able to witness myself getting plugged in, so I could stop and return to an open, more loving place. Instead of defending myself, I began to mirror what she was saying, and I saw her soften. She needed to be heard. Her feelings needed to be validated. She was best served by my love, not my resistance.

It's hard to show up with love for someone who's venting his or her anger or frustration, though. In some ways it's the ultimate spiritual challenge. I'm human, and when I get triggered, I can't help but react and my feelings rise quickly to the surface. That's when the real work begins. I need to step back, take a deep breath (or three), and put my ego aside. In this case, not only did I need to listen to my student with as much openness as possible, I needed to look at the role I played in our exchange during the workshop. Could I have been kinder? Was I too abrupt or impatient? If so, what was going on for me, and what do I need to do to take better care of myself?

As I sit here thinking about my conversation on the path, I'm reminded that we're all connected. We teach and learn, stumble and stand, and do our best to get through this crazy journey called life. I hope the woman I met feels better, and I hope the rest of the retreat goes smoothly.

March 8th

We're back from Arizona, and there's so much to process from last week. The retreat went well. Alanis, Michael, and I made a good team. The group was a great mix of loving, sensitive, creative people, most of whom were deeply grateful for the experience. Alanis is a natural wisdom teacher, the kind of presence we need in this world. She's a woman who's actually doing the work herself, who's unafraid of an emotionally charged process, who gives people back their power, and who's deeply committed to the evolution of her own soul.

She did a beautiful piece of healing work with Robin during a discussion about the stages of early development. Alanis was explaining the importance of receiving regular touch as a child because it gives us a palpable sense of existing in the world. She walked up behind Robin and ran her hands up and down Robin's arms as she talked, and I could see Robin melt into the moment. Alanis became a powerful embodiment of the Divine Mother, an archetypal energy that healed not only something in Robin, but in everyone who witnessed their exchange.

Michael was the perfect complementary masculine presence. His contributions were strong, yet unconditionally loving, and always considered. His event on Tuesday night where he offered intuitive readings to the group left us all shaking our heads in amazement. The level of detail he receives during readings is truly extraordinary—describing a woman's dog that had died and nearly getting the dog's name correct (he said Rosie and it was Josie), drawing an accurate picture of a woman's home in the Australian outback, or telling another woman she would buy land in Hawaii when it turned out she was in the process of arranging the purchase. Nearly every person Michael read for said, "Everything you've told me makes sense."

I sat in the back of the room with Ellen, and we were both astounded by Michael's amazing accuracy. When he was finished, someone asked him how he was able to read so clearly. Michael was quiet for a long moment before saying, "I'm not quite sure. All I know is that I tune in to love, I do my best to get my ego out of the way, and then I say whatever comes to me."

I was so proud of him, and I feel thankful to be married to such a good man.

March 9th

What a morning. I woke and found a post on Facebook from a different retreat participant who left a rant saying I was rude and unkind. Not the best way to start the day. When people splash their anger on the walls of a public forum rather than communicating with me directly (and privately), it strikes me as emotionally violent—and manipulative. While I was reading and rereading the post (hoping that it would magically transform into something positive), I felt heat rise from my stomach to my face, and I did my best to put a name to the feelings . . .

Embarrassment.

Guilt for hurting someone's feelings.

Shame.

Humiliation.

I lay in bed racking my brain to remember the exchange, but I couldn't come up with any recollection of the person or the encounter. I felt awful and pretty worked up, so I can't believe that after deleting the post, I was able to fall back to sleep. That's when something magical happened.

For the first time since her death, Debbie Ford came to me in a dream. I didn't see her, but I sensed her presence and I heard her voice.

"You are rude, Cheryl. And you're bitchy, too. And while we're at it, sometimes you can be short with people, and critical, and abrupt in ways that hurt."

I listened as she filled my consciousness with her words.

"Until you can embrace this truth about yourself, you'll always be afraid of hearing it from others. Remember, each of us embodies every quality; we are all everything. It's what you can't be with that won't let you be."

I woke from the dream feeling a wave of cool relief wash over me. Debbie was right. I am all of those things mentioned in the Facebook post *and* by the woman at Miraval. I am abrupt, and impatient, and too quick to cut people off sometimes, especially under the pressure of managing a large group experience. And while I would never intentionally hurt anyone, the truth is that I sometimes do.

There you have it.

It's not easy to look at the unattractive parts of ourselves. They feel shameful and embarrassing. But face them and embrace them we must if we're committed to walking a conscious path, and I am. It helps to think of life as a school. From this perspective, everything holds an opportunity for healing, an invitation to love and accept myself (and others) more.

I have to be honest. I'm no longer interested in being the Queen of Nice. It's exhausting. I'm more interested in being myself—all of me—good and bad, light and dark, kind and crappy. And if I hurt someone along the way, I'm truly sorry. I'm a work in progress, too. And as a work in progress, I'll make an effort to be more aware of my rough edges.

After the dream I felt so much better, relieved actually. Embracing the truth releases anxiety and quiets the harsh voice in my head.

Thank you, my dear Debbie. Thank you for supporting me, even from the other side. I miss you, dear friend. Every. Single. Day.

March 10th

I saw Sylvia this afternoon. We talked about the retreat and my experience teaching in Arizona, and how I continue to grapple with this shift that's taking place within me. Even this event, one I love, doesn't feel the same anymore. I'm not sure what does, and that makes me nervous. For years I've enjoyed creating a safe place for people to tell the truth about their lives. I've found it profoundly satisfying to hold people, to support them as they make important changes in their lives. If I'm not hosting events like this, what will I do?

The even bigger question is, who will I be? That's scarier. I'm changing in ways I don't fully understand. The familiar role of caregiver, confidant, mother, and champion seems to be molting like last year's skin, and I have no idea what will take its place. Fortunately this past year has taught me a lot about moving into unknown territory. This is a time to pay close attention to how I *feel*. What grabs me and holds my interest? What gives me energy? What makes me feel excited and alive?

Here's what I do know: I want to be patient, and to leave space for new people, ideas, experiences, and creative activities to reach out and find me. I don't want to chase life anymore. I want to feel pulled toward something.

Sylvia, in her wisdom, pointed out the link between my desire to put healthy limits on my giving to others and my last regression where I was a mother who couldn't feed her child. Her insight hit home. I no longer feel the need to do penance for the death of my little girl. Reliving the experience released me, and now I'm free to live without those historical constraints.

Later in our session, Sylvia and I used an inner process to explore the wisdom contained in that last past-life regression, and to imagine what might lie on the horizon. I saw myself sitting on the peak of a snow-covered mountain. The words *I'm hungry* came into my mind, and I started to cry. I've spent years, maybe my whole life, starving myself, and as I settled into this awareness, the truth bypassed my head and landed solidly in my body. I need to feed myself. I've been hungry for a long, long time.

I thought once again about what I'm hungry for: being at Miraval as a guest, not a teacher; unstructured days with time to myself; pleasure; leisurely shopping; traveling with Michael purely for the joy of it, not just to bring him along while I work; being a student myself and investing in the next stage of my own growth; welcoming friends to stay at the house without the hassle of working around my complicated schedule. As I considered these desires, I felt a familiar resistance rise up at the prospect of making pleasure more of a priority in this next stage of my life. It's just not in my DNA. I'm the daughter of an Irishman who has modeled the importance of sacrifice and the value of hard work. And I've been following in his footsteps since I was fourteen years old. I know how to push. I know how to perform. I know how to make things happen. Especially for other people.

Sylvia guided me to welcome in this part of me that's uncomfortable with the idea of focusing on my own pleasure. I put my hand on my heart and instantly felt connected to the precocious teenage girl who's frightened at the thought of standing still. I encouraged her to speak. *You've already lived an amazing life,* she tells me. *What more could you possibly want? It's not safe to slow down, and it's certainly not spiri-*

tual to focus on yourself. What if people judge you? What if you put your financial security at risk? What if you become overindulgent or lazy?

What if? What if? What if? Those two little words have kept me from doing what I long to do, and it needs to stop. Now I'm learning to feed myself.

When I tell my inner teenager that it's alright, that it's okay for us to stop for a while and consider what we need to feel happy and at peace, I can feel her surrender just a little. She needs to take a nap and let me run the show.

March 13th

It's been a full-on day. I was up early to get my hair done before leaving tomorrow for Toronto to give a speech, one of the few left before I take a break from travel for a while. Around noontime, I discovered a technical glitch with the online course I'm doing with Hay House, and I spent the next hour working it out with the team before driving into the city.

This afternoon I attended an angel-investment summit in Boston, to get an update on some of the companies Michael and I have invested in, and by the time I drove home from the city, I was exhausted. After dinner, I came here to bed and now intend to fall fast asleep.

March 15th

I just finished my talk this morning in Toronto, came back to the hotel to enjoy a cup of tea, and now I'm going out for a long walk. I'm off in search of a foot massage in Chinatown. I'm so glad I packed my sneakers for this trip. I almost left them at home, thinking they would take up unnecessary space in my overnight bag, but after making a point of being active every day, it has become a priority. Thankfully.

Later

Back from a walk in the cold, windy weather here in the city. The sun was doing its best to peek through the clouds outside my hotel window, so the day looked much warmer than it actually was. I went all the way down to Chinatown and found a place to get a foot massage, but it only accepted cash and I hadn't notified my bank about traveling outside the country, so I couldn't use my ATM card. Too bad. But at least I got in a good, long walk.

When I returned to my hotel, I began answering email; then I looked over at the end of the bed and noticed the sun had cast a pool of light across the comforter. *I'd love to curl up right there and take a nap,* I thought, but I continued working. Responding to others' requests and ignoring my own. *I have to be somewhere in an hour,* I told myself. *I don't have time for a nap.*

That's when I stopped typing. *Wouldn't the warmth of the sun feel good, Cheryl? Why aren't you listening to your own needs?* So I put down my computer, grabbed a pillow, and curled up on the comforter. I lay there feeling the warmth on my face as clouds floated by, playing hide-and-seek with the sun. I imagined myself lying on a beach, carefree and happy, soaking in the pleasures of this moment.

Thank you, I said to myself as I drifted off to sleep.

It's been too easy to make efficiency and checking off a list more important than living my life, but these days I'm doing a better job of not waiting for *someday.* I'm serving a new master—one who is loving and sane, sensitive and smart. And guess what? I'm still alive. No lightning bolts from above. No one has died. Everything that matters is getting done, and all in the right way, at the right time.

Who knew?

March 16th

I'm sitting in Toronto's Billy Bishop Airport waiting to board a flight home. Across from me, a dad plays with a little boy sitting in his lap who looks to be about a year old. The young father speaks softly to his son as he carefully removes his coat, kissing him on the top of his head. I notice that both dad and son have Buddhist prayer beads wrapped around their wrists.

This is one of those moments when the grief of not having children could reduce me to a puddle of tears right here in the gate area of this airport. Today I know that I would parent my child like this father. I would be gentle and kind and loving to both my child and myself. But I didn't know that long ago. I didn't trust myself. So I allow the sadness to be present while doing my best to keep it together—the delicate duet of feeling and existing in the world.

Later

As I got up to leave the lounge to get on the plane, the father and his child joined the line for my flight, and the strangest thing happened. Once on board, I watched the young man stow his carry-on under the seat while balancing his boy on his hip. Then he began to gently rock his son on his shoulder in a way I knew I'd seen before. That's when it hit me: This was the same dad I'd seen a year ago while traveling to Toronto for last year's Hay House conference. I remember watching him walk up and down the aisle of the plane, smiling and cooing at his newborn baby. The same grief stabbed my heart then, too, and I had to work hard to keep the floodgates in place.

This young man and his child evoke a tender dimension of parenthood that Michael and I rarely factored into our discussions when we were considering having children. For many years we only heard about the challenges of being parents—kids are such a huge responsibility, you never stop worrying about them, it costs so much money to raise a child, etc. Our decision not to become parents, while made consciously, was influenced more by our concerns about what could go wrong than what could be right.

I can't imagine that seeing this father and his little boy is a coincidence. How strange that one year later they would show up again. This man is revealing the beauty of an intimate love I'll never know, and it feels like an invitation to grieve a little more. After all, the decision to not have children is no small matter—it's a choice worthy of grief. Feeling the pain of this loss is healing and necessary. It seems my heart must continually break to allow more love in.

March 17th

Today a herd of deer (I count ten) has been grazing on the newly exposed grass outside the house. They are such exquisite creatures—gray winter coats soon to be tan, black noses testing the breeze, cautious eyes and ears scanning for movement. I see them drift from one spot to the next, heads bent to the ground one moment, then up and alert to danger the next.

As I watch them eat, I think about my own hunger. While winter is normally a time for hibernation, I feel like I've been waking up. The decision to surrender to the mystery, to a future unknown, has taught me so much about what I need to feed my own soul. *Eat up my friends,* I tell the deer telepathically. *Fill your bellies. Thank you for being here.*

While they may not hear my words, I have no doubt they feel the energy of my love.

March 19th

Tomorrow is the first day of spring, and it can't come soon enough. This morning the outside thermometer registered ten degrees—while it's still too cold, the good news is that with all the snow we've had, the reservoir will be filled to capacity. Just two years ago, there was so little rain and snow that some twenty feet of shoreline was exposed, prompting concerns about drought. I get so much pleasure from our water view, and I know that so many birds and animals rely on it; it's good to know it's being replenished.

My friend and fellow angel investor, John, came to visit this week, and we had lunch with the principals of a company we've counseled and helped to finance. We celebrated a milestone with the CEO and COO, and then came back to the house to work out in the gym with Michael before going to dinner. I love that our home has become the welcoming self-care haven we always hoped it would be.

From the first day Michael and I started building it more than eight years ago, we held the intention that we would honor this land by creating a peaceful home that offered healing to everyone who passed over the threshold. I'll never forget walking through the opening of what would eventually become our front door and finding the framers sitting on the first-floor deck. They were lined up in a row, feet dangling off the edge of the back wall, looking out over the water while eating their lunch. It was freezing cold that day, and they each had a lunch bag on one side and a steaming thermos on the other. Hats and gloves and warm clothes covered everything but their faces. I felt bad for them working in such harsh conditions, yet when they turned around to greet me they were all grinning from ear to ear.

"This is one beautiful place you have here," said the foreman, as he bit off a piece of his sandwich.

I smiled and thought to myself, *It's working already.*

March 20th

I woke to gray skies hanging low over the reservoir this morning, but they can't dampen my mood. It's the first day of spring, and I couldn't be happier. As I walk around the house looking out at the bare magnolia tree that will be one of the first to bloom, I feel my body smile. Spring opens a doorway to possibility. There's a deck garden to plan, birdhouses to clear, and the anticipation of a gangly, delicate fawn emerging from the fields, cautiously stepping into new life.

I can feel myself releasing some of the fear of the unknown, the inner turmoil, the angst of lingering in limbo. I'm ready to cull the wisdom of winter in order to set the stage for the new beginnings that lie ahead. As I read back over these pages, I'm glad I took the time to record this period in my life. Writing not only works to stem the tide of forgetting, but it also offers me the clarity that only hindsight can deliver.

In these pages, I see a woman moving as if through a fog, groping for something solid to hold on to as she navigates an unfamiliar season—the autumn of life. This is a time of reflection, a time to harvest life experiences, lessons learned, and the wisdom gained from both success and failure. In some ways I've taken on the classic hero's journey, or heroine's journey in this case. The voyage begins with a call for something more, something deeper and more aligned with who we really are. This beckons us down, down, down, descending into unknown places where what we've always done no longer works. Once here, we are released into the mystery, and here we remain, not knowing why or for how long.

If we heed the call and hold on through the darkness, the ascent begins. And that's where I find myself now. There's a metamorphosis under way, and while I'm not sure who or what will emerge from the chrysalis, here's what I do know:

> Sometimes the best way to discover what really matters is to release what doesn't, and see what's left behind.

> I can't live a new life with an old version of me. In order to live consciously and to keep growing, I must be willing to dismantle some aspects of the identity that has brought me to this point in my life without knowing who, or what, will take its place.

> I must tend to my inner life like I do my garden— with consistent attention and loving care. My inner life must now be granted equal weight with my outer life.

> I must honor my soul's need for space. My version of a good life requires that I have the freedom and openness in my schedule to cultivate a state of presence and to live more spontaneously.

> The life I've hungered for was waiting for me; I just needed to stop long enough to notice. It turns

out that what matters most is what I'm blessed to already have: a good husband, loving friends and family, the beauty in and around our home, the wildlife that fills me with such joy, and the peace and comfort to be found in a daily routine.

As I emerge from this winter with a greater understanding of myself and of my needs, I do so with a grateful heart. I'm getting ready to free myself from the chrysalis, and I'm excited to see what life has in store. I also offer my gratitude to May Sarton, whose inspiration led me here in the first place. In addition to all that I've learned, I've confirmed for myself a realization she came to in her *Journal of a Solitude* so long ago.

"So perhaps we write toward what we will become from where we are," Sarton declares in her final entry.

Perhaps we do.

A Special Message
to the Reader

Dear Friend,

Midlife can be both an exciting and challenging time. Our willingness to engage in a thoughtful and deliberate process of inquiry at this stage can mean the difference between a meaningful and mediocre life. To inspire a useful reckoning, I've designed a series of questions for you to answer on your own, in a journal, or with a group. Self-awareness is a catalyst for growth and positive change. Be brave and please take your time. The answers to these questions will support the kind of midlife introspection that can bring peace and clarity to the choices you make in the next exciting season of your life.

In addition to the questions, I've also added a resource section that includes some of the books, movies, websites, and so on that are mentioned throughout these pages, as well as additional favorites that I've found comforting and helpful.

- If you were to give your life thus far a title, what would that title be? Why?

- What has life taught you about yourself?

- If your life were to end today, what would you regret? What would you regret not having done? Who would you regret not having become?

- Think of life as a school. What lessons have shaped the person you are today? What have you learned about how life works?

- What are the top five priorities worthy of your time and attention? What makes them worthy?

- What do you need to release from your life in order to make space for the priorities that matter now? What would you let go of if you knew you could do so without negative consequences?

- If you were to give your identity an upgrade, what qualities of character would you add, change, or strengthen in order to live a more conscious and authentic life? What aspects of your identity would you release?

- How will you tend to your inner life?

- What's great about your life right now? Where do you find meaning or feel a sense of purpose? Who are you grateful for and why?

- What are the simple pleasures that give you a deep sense of joy and satisfaction?

- If you were to receive an award for doing what you most enjoy, what would the award be called? Why?

- If life gives us messages (before lessons, problems, and crises), what messages might life be sending you now? How are you responding to these messages?

- Think of someone whose behavior feels frustrating or upsetting (from your past or present). What is it about the behavior that causes you discomfort? What aspect of your identity might he or she be inviting you to embrace? What might he or she be trying to teach you about yourself?

- How have the tribes that you belong to (family, school groups, religious communities, friends, work colleagues, and the like) influenced who you've become and the choices you've made in your life? Which tribes support your authentic expression now? Which tribes suppress it?

- What do you keep looking forward to? If you were to move your future into the present, how would you live your life differently?

- If your body could talk, what would it say about your life thus far?

- Name five of your most treasured memories. What makes them memorable? What do these experiences have to teach you about what matters most at this time in your life?

Resources

Audio Programs

Experience the Power of Grace by Cheryl Richardson

Finding Your Passion by Cheryl Richardson

The Enneagram by Helen Palmer

Sitting by the Well: Bringing the Feminine to Consciousness Through Language, Dreams, and Metaphor by Marion Woodman

The Crown of Age by Marion Woodman

Holding the Tension of Opposites by Marion Woodman

Books

You Can Create An Exceptional Life by Cheryl Richardson and Louise Hay

The Art of Extreme Self-Care: Transform Your Life One Month at a Time by Cheryl Richardson

The Unmistakable Touch of Grace: How to Recognize and Respond to the Spiritual Signposts in Your Life by Cheryl Richardson

Stand Up for Your Life: A Practical Step-by-Step Plan to Build Inner Confidence and Personal Power by Cheryl Richardson

Life Makeovers: 52 Practical & Inspiring Ways to Improve Your Life One Week at a Time by Cheryl Richardson

Take Time for Your Life: A Personal Coach's 7-Step Program for Creating the Life You Want by Cheryl Richardson

The Highly Sensitive Person: How to Thrive When the World Overwhelms You by Elaine N. Aron, Ph.D.

A Woman's Journey to God: Finding the Feminine Path by Joan Borysenko, Ph.D.

The Hero's Journey: Joseph Campbell on His Life and Work by Joseph Campbell

Courage: Overcoming Fear & Igniting Self-Confidence by Debbie Ford

The Dark Side of the Light Chasers: Reclaiming Your Power, Creativity, Brilliance, and Dreams by Debbie Ford

When the Heart Waits: Spiritual Direction for Life's Sacred Questions by Sue Monk Kidd

Life Loves You: 7 Spiritual Practices to Heal Your Life by Louise Hay and Robert Holden

Red Moon Passage: The Power and Wisdom of Menopause by Bonnie J. Horrigan

Balancing Heaven and Earth: A Memoir of Visions,
*   Dreams, and Realizations* by Robert A. Johnson
Goddesses Never Age: The Secret Prescription for
*   Radiance, Vitality, and Well-Being* by Christiane
    Northrup, M.D.
The Wisdom of Menopause: Creating Physical and
*   Emotional Health During the Change* (revised edition)
    by Christiane Northrup, M.D.
Women's Bodies, Women's Wisdom: Creating Physical
*   and Emotional Health and Healing* (revised edition) by
    Christiane Northrup M.D.
New and Selected Poems, Volume One by Mary Oliver
Molecules of Emotion: The Science Behind Mind-Body
*   Medicine* by Candace B. Pert, Ph.D.
The Wisdom of the Enneagram: The Complete Guide
*   to Psychological and Spiritual Growth for the Nine*
*   Personality Types* by Don Richard Riso and Russ
    Hudson
The Enneagram Made Easy: Discover the 9 Types of People
    by Renee Baron and Elizabeth Wagele
Women Food and God: An Unexpected Path to Almost
*   Everything* by Geneen Roth
Journal of a Solitude by May Sarton
The House by the Sea: A Journal by May Sarton
Encore: A Journal of the Eightieth Year by May Sarton
Many Lives, Many Masters: The True Story of a Prominent
*   Psychiatrist, His Young Patient, and the Past-Life*

Therapy That Changed Both Their Lives by Brian L. Weiss, M.D.

Miracles Happen: The Transformational Healing Power of Past-Life Memories by Brian L. Weiss, M.D., and Amy E. Weiss, MSW

Bone: Dying into Life by Marion Woodman

Autobiography of a Yogi by Paramahansa Yogananda

Card Decks

My Daily Affirmation Cards: A 50-Card Deck by Cheryl Richardson

Grace Cards: A 50-Card Deck by Cheryl Richardson

Self-Care Cards: A 52-Card Deck by Cheryl Richardson

Films

Romeo & Juliet (2013) Starring Damian Lewis, Douglas Booth, and Hailee Steinfeld

Before Sunrise (1995) Starring Ethan Hawke and Julie Delpy

Before Sunset (2004) Starring Ethan Hawke and Julie Delpy

The Secret Life of Walter Mitty (2013) Starring Ben Stiller and Kristen Wiig

The Power of Myth with Bill Moyers, 25th Anniversary Edition

Online Courses

The Art of Extreme Self-Care: Transform Your Life One Month at a Time by Cheryl Richardson (available at HayHouse.com)

Websites

Alanis.com: Official website for Alanis Morissette.

MichaelGerrish.com: Official website for Michael Gerrish.

AnimalSpirit.org: Official website for animal communicator Anna Breytenbach.

CoachFederation.org: International Coach Federation, the largest independent professional organization for professional coaches worldwide. Includes information on becoming a coach as well as a coach referral service.

CompassionPower.com: Books and programs for couples from Steven Stosny, Ph.D.

EnneagramInstitute.com: Riso–Hudson Enneagram Type Indicator test.

HarvilleAndHelen.com: Books, DVDs, programs, and workshops for couples from Harville Hendrix, Ph.D., and Helen LaKelly Hunt, Ph.D.

cirillocompany.de/pages/pomodoro-technique: Official website of the Pomodoro Technique®, a time-management method developed by Francesco Cirillo, named after the tomato-shaped kitchen timer that he used as a university student.

UnderstandMen.com: Books, DVDs, programs, and coaching for men and women in relationships from Alison Armstrong.

Acknowledgments

Every artist needs loving support to help quiet the critical voices that threaten the creative process. I've been blessed with an abundance of such support, and for that I'm deeply grateful.

My heartfelt thanks to Marilyn Abraham, who has been with me from the beginning and always kicks off a new project with humor and good sense; to my personal editor, Peter Guzzardi, for encouraging me to be patient and for helping me to bring more truth and beauty to my writing; and to Ellen Wingard, whose poetic wisdom gave me direction and courage when I needed it most.

To my editor at HarperOne, Gideon Weil, thank you for responding with lightning speed, for sharing my vision, for offering wise guidance along the way, and for patiently waiting a decade. You've been a joy. And to my sweet sister Debbie Ford, for working your magic from the other side.

Many thanks to the behind-the-scene angels at HarperOne: Mary Grangeia, Adrian Morgan, Alex Potter, and Ralph Fowler (SBI), for your artistry and attention to detail.

A deep bow to the friends and fellow writers who read early versions of this book and provided helpful feedback and encouragement: Donna Abate, Carol Davis, Susan Doughty, Russ Hudson, Alanis Morissette, Kamal Ravikant, Kerri Richardson, Anna Robertson, Ernest and Kerrin Thompson, Michelle Tomaso, Liz Trubridge, Meggan Watterson, and Amy Weiss.

Thank you to Amanda Urban for your honesty and encouragement, Reid Tracy for your helpful feedback, Mark Lawless for always having my back, Shannon Littrell for your good heart and editing prowess, and Scott Richardson for the fun adventure while taking the cover photo.

My heartfelt gratitude goes to the team who supports me and my work, and protects the space I need to write: Chris Barnes, Robin and Larry Gillette, Terry Nolan, and Nicole Paull. You all mean the world to me.

Thank you to Sylvia Hammerman for your loving presence and for helping me to find the light in the darkness; to Rita Heron for your sharp mind and no-nonsense wise counsel; and to my soul family Bob and Melissa Olson, Ileen Maisel, Nanna Aida Svendsen, Kelly O'Brien, and Bruce Kohl. Every writer should be so lucky to have champions like you.

And finally, to my husband, Michael Gerrish. Thank you for your wisdom, your unwavering support, your valuable editorial feedback, and for allowing me to share some of the intimate details of our marriage. I don't know how I'd survive here without you.

About the Author

Cheryl Richardson is the *New York Times* bestselling author of *Take Time for Your Life, Life Makeovers, Stand Up for Your Life, The Unmistakable Touch of Grace, The Art of Extreme Self-Care,* and *You Can Create an Exceptional Life* with Louise Hay. She hosts a large online community at cherylrichardson.com, Facebook.com/CherylRichardson, and on Twitter and Instagram under the user name coachoncall. These communities are dedicated to helping people around the world improve their quality of life.